M000247556

PORTMEIRION

Jan Morris, Alwyn W Turner,
Mark Eastment, Stephen Lacey and Robin Llywelyn,
FOREWORD BY Jools Holland
SPECIAL GARDEN PHOTOGRAPHY BY Charles Hawes

ANTIQUE COLLECTORS' CLUB

CONTENTS

Exhilarated by my vision, I wander on, imagining so many citizens having my sort of dreams that one day they resolve to see them actually realized – CLOUGH WILLIAMS-ELLIS, 1971

INSPIRED BY CLOUGH

Jools Holland

ABOVE: The gold medal-winning Portmeirion garden at Chelsea Flower Show in 1999 with (right) Jools Holland pictured inside the tower that he subsequently relocated to his studio in Greenwich, London.

It was the TV series *The Tube* that first took me to Portmeirion. I was one of the presenters of the show, and we decided to do a spoof of *The Prisoner* and have various bands playing in the village. I'd seen the original Patrick McGoohan series as a child, of course, and - quite apart from it being an intriguing, enigmatic story - I remember being mystified by why someone would want to escape from such a charming looking place.

I was already interested in architecture - my favourite toy had been Lego bricks, and my father used to take me to St Paul's Cathedral and to see other great buildings - but it was Portmeirion that re-fired my enormous enthusiasm for the subject. Once there, I realized that it was the place itself that was so exciting. I had no idea how enchanting and utterly beautiful it would be, and I actually found myself running around like a happy child.

As I pursued this initial interest and began reading about Clough Williams-Ellis, I discovered that the more I found out about him, the more I liked him. I loved the way he thought, the way he approached things, the way he wasn't afraid to use the motif of light opera: architecture didn't have to be po-faced or uncomfortable or brutal, it can be friendly and welcoming. His ethos was simple

but inspiringly so. When you look at a building, he wrote, you've got to ask it a number of questions. One, does it keep the rain and the wind out, are the inhabitants comfortable? Two, did the person who designed the building think that it was beautiful? Three, do I, the viewer, find the building beautiful?

He believed that once you have the vocabulary of architecture and an awareness of composition, then you can start to have fun with it; that's when you can fly. And you can see exactly that exuberance in his work.

For me, the great realization in this was that Clough is probably the most musical of architects. And he was musical too in his attitude that that you can take from anywhere, you can borrow from anything - all great music takes and borrows themes and styles and mixes it all up. There aren't any hard and fast rules, as long as the end result has a pleasing effect. Clough does that more than any other architect, and yet every time you see one of his buildings, you recognize it as being undeniably him. If you're a musician, you want to have your own sound, and as an architect he very definitely had his own look. He managed to capture elegance and he took such pleasure in doing it.

In great music, there is always something new to be discovered - new mysteries appear in pieces that you think you know, new aspects to be explored. Clough and his work is like that: there always seemed to be something new for him to learn, something new to invent. And often it's the bits that are almost thrown away, the way he'd sketch something up on a doorway, that are most striking. It's the composition that's truly inspiring, while so much of contemporary architecture is based solely on purpose, no composition is involved. In composition, in style, in the proportions of his buildings, he is as great as - if not greater than - any of his contemporaries.

You can see so much of this at Portmeirion. The buildings are put together like the most beautiful music or the most beautiful paintings.

Above all, he genuinely cared about people, about the welfare of his fellow man. I think he would have happily lived in anything he built. His buildings weren't for profit alone; he was always asking whether a building would make people's lives better, would it cheer them up and enchant them.

The more I read, the more I identified with Clough. He gave up his formal training very early, and he always said that he wasn't a man for sitting on committees. I too am not professionally trained either as an architect or as a musician, but - as he showed - the only qualification you need is actually to build something: it's about the joy of doing it. He was largely self-taught, and that's the best way of learning anything. You have to be taught the principles by someone else, but what you really learn from is experience and a love of the subject. My friend, Candida Lycett-Green, says she remembers him being asked what the precise measurements were of one of his pieces, and him replying: 'Just use your eyes; just look at it and use your eyes.'

These were the lessons that Clough taught me and that inspired me when I began designing my studio and its surrounding buildings in the mid-'90s. I wasn't trying to copy Clough, but instead to capture some of the atmosphere of his work. It's on a smaller scale, of course, and it's located in London, but the notion is the same - the intention of creating something enchanting and magical, to lift the human spirit a bit and to make people feel like they're on holiday.

Each time I go to Portmeirion, I see something new. I'll find a detail, a little throwaway ornament, maybe a cartouche that he took from Inigo Jones and that he reproduced in concrete and render, and it's a new inspiration - you look at it and you think: I could make one of those. Clough made architecture accessible.

And he made Portmeirion, a magical, romantic place. You get the impression that even in his own time, Clough was from another age, and Portmeirion has the charm and elegance of a bygone time.

Jools Holland

Clough Williams-Ellis was his own best work,

splendid in all proportions – THE TIMES, 1978

CLOUGH'S SHANGRI-LA
Jan Morris

LEFT: Portmeirion
with Snowdon in the
background from
across the Dwyryd
Estuary.

RIGHT: Portrait of Clough
by Hans Feibusch
(1898-1998). Pencil
on paper. Feibusch
painted several
Baroque murals and
metal cut-outs for
Clough at Portmeirion.

If you drive up the north-western coast of Wales towards the mountains of Eryri – Snowdonia to the English – somewhere around Harlech, at longitude 52.52N, latitude 04.07W, you may see something extraordinary.

Across the water, on the other side of the Dwyryd Estuary, there stands an isolated cluster of buildings that suggests at first sight some kind of hallucination. It seems separate from the landscape all around it, the wooded hills immediately behind, the severely noble mountains beyond, the general sense of magnificent austerity that attends this corner of Wales. Its colours are not muted, as one expects them to be. Its silhouettes look decidedly festive. It is not in the least restrained. Could it be some aristocratic folly? Or might it be just a dream?

It is both. It is a patrician folly-dream. It is the *village fantastique* called Portmeirion, created from scratch, eight decades ago, by a visionary Welsh landowner and architect who even made up a name for it.

RIGHT: Clough's preliminary plan for Portmeirion, drawn in 1925 to attract financial backers, and (opposite) Portmeirion as actually built.

Clough Willams-Ellis was the son of a local Welsh squarson – at once a landed gentleman and an Anglican clergyman (and a poet too, as it happened). He was named after paternal family connections in Denbighshire, and from his boyhood he was known to everyone in the neighbourhood simply as Clough. Twenty years after his death, so he is remembered still.

Born in 1883, he went to an English public school, fought in the First World War, inherited the family estates and became a kind of architect – 'kind of', because in fact he had no professional qualifications, and conducted a successful and fashionable practice simply by talent, charm and chutzpah. He prospered in London, married a wife from the eminently politico-literary Strachey family, designed buildings of many kinds in many parts of Britain, but was drawn back always to his native corner of Wales, where the mountains of Eryri come down to the sea. There, in the 1920s, he invented Portmeirion.

F R O M · T H E · S E A   F R O M · T H E · L A N D

ABOVE: Clough's earliest surviving design for Portmeirion, c.1925 (detail), showing an irregular group of cliff top structures including a bell tower and cottages. Pen with pencil corrections on linen (545x775mm).

LEFT: Clough in his characteristic outfit in the Mirror Room of the Hotel Portmeirion and (right) at his drawing board in the Library at Plas Brondanw.

Clough was a friend and neighbour of mine for forty years, and the longer I knew him the more I realized that Portmeirion, his idiosyncratic masterpiece, was his own exact representation. It was himself in stone, in colour, in fun, in purpose and most of all in imagination. Nobody was ever more individualist, and just as Portmeirion, whether you like it or not, is impossible to dismiss, so Clough for all his faults was unforgettable too.

He looked, I always thought, like an extremely entertaining horse. His figure was bony, his face was long, his nose was protuberant, his gait was lanky and when he laughed (as he very frequently did) his big front teeth were decidedly equine. He wore long yellow stockings with breeches, flamboyant waistcoats, bright bow ties. He never seemed to change much, during my acquaintance with him, and in my memory he was at his most characteristic when he was stooped over a stand-up drawing-board in the study at Plas Brondanw, his family home a few miles inland from Portmeirion. His humour was simple, and infectious. His tastes in art, literature and architecture were essentially conservative. He loved to boast of his immemorial paternal ancestry among the princes of northern Wales, and he was by no means unconscious of his own attractions.

ABOVE: The Piazza with
the Bristol Colonnade in
the foreground.

But he was full of surprise. For a start there was his marriage to Amabel Strachey. Almost by inheritance she was a fervent socialist, a true London society intellectual of the 1920s, almost a blue-stocking, daunting to frivolous folk and antipathetic one might suppose to a merry traditionalist like Clough. In fact they lived in perfect harmony, so far as I know, until the day he died, producing a son and two daughters and collaborating on several books – including, since they were addicts of anomaly, the official history of the Royal Tank Regiment in the First World War. Later there was to grow up around Clough and Amabel, in their then remote and romantic demesne, a curiously assorted coterie of friends, some permanently resident, some with second homes there: scientists, artists, writers, mostly of left-wing political persuasion, many very distinguished, none of them bores.

It was a kind of Arcadia that the Willams-Ellises created, so it was natural that Arcadianism became Clough's chief preoccupation. He was not an advanced or even progressive sort of architect. His early work was recognizably of the Arts and

Crafts movement, it ended with tentative essays in 1930s modernism, but at heart he really admired nothing more recent than the Georgian, and almost all his designs were retrospective. He had an inborn eye, though, doubtless inherited from generations of his landowning ancestry, for the look of the landscape. He hated to see it degraded by the inroads of industry, and more particularly by the threat of mass tourism, and he became an early practitioner of the newly recognized branch of architecture called Town Planning.

He and Amabel became pioneers in the infant conservation movement. They published books and pamphlets. They addressed meetings. They added their names to petitions. They sat on innumerable committees. They were early supporters of national parks, and of the National Trust. Clough's whimsical and oddly innocent sense of humour, allied to Amabel's fierce sense of social justice, made their voices well-known and influential wherever the future of the environment was debated, and of course it was inevitable that the future of their own corner of Wales entered largely into their thoughts.

LEFT: Clough and Amabel picnicking on the Portmeirion peninsula, 1962.

OPPOSITE: The Hotel lawn with its original Victorian balustrade and Coade stone statues and view up towards the Village.

The Snowdon mountains, and the countryside around them, had been tourist destinations for years, but mostly of a dilettante kind. Lovers of the picturesque, botanists, artists, scholarly mountain-climbers, amateurs of history or of language – these were the sort of travellers who had for generations been finding their way to Clough's part of Wales. The tourist industry. such as it was, was a matter of cottage teas and simple lodgings, and people wrote books about their exotic adventures among the peaks and peasants of wild Wales, and its unpronounceable native language.

Like most other Welsh gentry of his day, Clough spoke no Welsh: but by his time it was all too obvious that tourism was about to threaten the very nature of his country – including, in the long run, its language. The first railways reached Snowdonia in the 1840s, bringing with them the first-comers of modern, populist tourism. A century later the automobile brought thousands more, and tourism became a mammoth growth industry, bringing with it all its ancillaries of commerce, second homes, alien ways and profitable vulgarity.

Clough, it seems, wanted to set a local example which might have a universal effect upon these developments. He determined to build a tourist resort on his own doorstep which would in no way harm its environment, whether physical or metaphysical – would not wreck the landscape, would not weaken the Welshness of its society, would encourage a love of beauty among its visitors and might encourage commercial developers to temper their profits with sympathy for local concerns.

That at least is how he recalled it all in retrospect, and no doubt Amabel encouraged such worthy motives. Remembering Clough's gift of high spirits, though, bearing in mind his yellow stockings, his bow ties and his irrepressible laughter, for myself I cannot help thinking that he invented Portmeirion largely for the fun of it. The spot where he built it, a small peninsula on the coast of Meirionnydd, already had a name, Aber Iâ: but since this apparently meant Estuary Of Ice, or something of the sort, he concocted Portmeirion instead (but was never quite sure how to pronounce it).

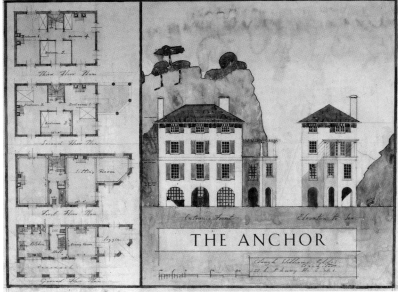

ABOVE LEFT: Clough's design for the Observatory Tower (1935) which incorporates a camera obscura. Pencil with coloured washes and watercolour (655x735mm).

ABOVE RIGHT: Clough's design for the Anchor (1930; built 1936) showing the dramatic setting. Pencil with coloured washes and watercolour on tracing paper (380x495mm).

If we drive round the head of the estuary, over its eponymous Dwyryd river, and follow the road to the west, we shall find a sign directing us to Portmeirion, painted in a slightly precious style and defining the place as an 'Italianate Village'.

Well, I suppose it partly is, but it is far more than that. Consider the approach: We pass beneath a sort of Gothic gatehouse, past a kind of gnome-like village green, beneath a variety of Baroque houses, alongside a Regency-looking colonnade, beside some white-washed Cotswoldian cottages, with, yes, a distinctly Portofino-type campanile on a hillock to your left, through a neat little double row of shops and a restaurant, past what seems to be a Jacobean town hall, down an incline from where you can see across the water to our vantage point this morning, until we are debouched at the door of a white Welsh country house beside the golden sands of the estuary. It is like entering a man's imagination.

And that's only a first impression! The place is full of grace-notes and curiosities, memorials to grand summers of the past, dogs' graves left over from previous occupations, pillars, obelisks, ponds, *trompe l'oeils*, architectural jokes, historical allusions, the whole surrounded by woodland and bounded by a wild promontory into Bae Ceredigion, Cardigan Bay, where monkey-puzzle trees stand high above the sea like a copse on the Pacific. If it all seems a little too much, well, Clough was never one for modesty.

Besides, for once he was his own client. He was the architect, but he was also the patron, the builder, the landscape planner and the risk-taking developer. Portmeirion was entirely his! Later in life he was to be concerned with the English new towns, those innovative Government urban projects built after the Second World War, and intended to offer officially sponsored standards of life and society.

RIGHT: The view from outside the Town Hall through its wrought iron gates towards the Pantheon with its plywood dome (built 1960-61; dome rebuilt in copper 1992).

ABOVE: The Hotel in 1928 with the *Amis Réunis* moored at the quayside, with construction of Government House on the cliff top to the right.

Clough had built his own new town at a time when planning restrictions and bureaucratic controls were in their infancy; the sense of personal liberty, personal responsibility, personal taste and personal character was, for better as for worse, instinct in its every whim and cranny.

There was a time before the War when Portmeirion was essentially a holiday retreat for the upper classes, an exclusive sort of Shangri-la. Clough conceived it as an upmarket hotel with an attendant village – the hotel down at the water's edge, the village a trim collection of cottages that could be rented for long or short stays. It had a Cockpit Smoke Room built from the timbers of the last wooden warship of the Royal Navy to sail into action. It had a State Bedroom, decorated in grey-blue, jade green and old gold, in which the Prince of Wales stayed in 1934. Portmeirion then was an expensively homogenous little hideaway, its management gentlemanly, its posh clientele mostly from London and southern England – there was a satellite hotel, the Mytton and Mermaid near Shrewsbury, to offer a suitably civilized night's break on the long road up.

Toffs and celebrities of one sort and another, actors and dukes, philosophers and playwrights frequented the place. Clough preferred it that way. He had a weakness for the rich and famous, and admitted once to a distaste for regional accents. However he also intended from the start that his resort should make money. Day visitors were encouraged to visit, paying a sliding scale of entrance fees according to demand – the more people who wanted to see the place, the more they paid to get in, thus preserving both the amenities and the profits. The hotel itself was reserved for residents, and this seemed to work perfectly well, although Clough and Amabel

ABOVE: The Cockpit Bar in the Hotel, constructed from the timbers of HMS *Arethusa*, which was lost in the 1981 fire.

ABOVE RIGHT: The Mirror Room in the Hotel in the 1920s.

kept eagle eyes upon behaviour which might now be yobbish, but in those days seldom went further than taking cuttings from flower-beds.

The Second World War, though, which changed the nature of tourism, changed the nature of Portmeirion too. North Wales, which had once been a particular haunt of the grand, the fastidious and the eccentrically cultivated, swarmed now with holidaymakers from the English Midlands, from Merseyside and Manchester. The sort of people who came to Portmeirion before the war, to relax in its familiar kind of sophistication with the Noel Cowards and the Bertrand Russells, now more often went abroad. Regional accents sounded confidently in the hotel itself, and resounded boisterously through its village, its gardens, its sands and its ice-cream shops.

Whatever Clough thought of these societal changes, he was unperturbed. As he grew into old age, and became less concerned with his architectural practice, and more and more devoted to his private masterpiece, the more benignly he presided over it all, relishing the admiration alike of trippers, neighbours and connoisseurs as he strolled yellow-stockinged and cord-breeched through the estate.

Today it is not quite as he conceived it, nor precisely how seemed to us from the other side of the estuary. Twentieth-century Portmeirion is slicker, smoother and more commercial than it looks – or used to be.

An inescapable motif now is the heritage of a cult 1960s television series, *The Prisoner*, which was set and acted at Portmeirion. There is a quaint shop in the village dedicated to the memory of the series, devoted anoraks swarm in pilgrimage, and nowadays if ever Portmeirion enters a conversation, *The Prisoner*,

RIGHT: Lady's Lodge
(built 1938-39),
Portmeirion's last
pre-War building, with
Toll House behind.

ABOVE: Susan Williams-
Ellis' sheet metal cut-
out of a black sheep,
designed for the Welsh
wool shop in 1957,
now hanging from
Toll House.

not Clough, is liable to be the first thing mentioned. Or perhaps it may be Portmeirion Pottery, a delightful and authentically Williams-Ellis family brand which is produced in the English pottery town of Stoke-on-Trent, but is generally assumed throughout the civilized world to be made by traditional Welsh-speaking craftsmen in the woods above the estuary of the Dwyryd, where the mountains come down to the sea.

Yet in its essence Portmeirion has scarcely changed since Clough's time. The hodge-podge feel of it all, the exuberant mix of shapes and colours, its laughing style and hint of throw-away learning, is as seductive to some temperaments nowadays, and as unappealing to others, as ever it was in the 1930s. And run today by a family trust, managed by Clough's grandson Robin Llywelyn, the place is physically in better shape than ever.

This is partly because soon after Clough's death the hotel was burnt down, and has since been rebuilt in more or less its original form. Also a Victorian mock castle near the entrance to the estate, Castell Deudraeth, has been turned into an ancillary hotel and restaurant. The whole place has been, so to speak, rejuvenated with fresh paint and restoratives, and perhaps most tellingly of all Portmeirion has become decidedly more Welsh. Robin Llywelyn is not merely Welsh-speaking, he is perhaps the best-known and most innovative novelist writing in Welsh today, and he has integrated Portmeirion more thoroughly than ever into the life of contemporary Wales: most of Portmeirion's staff are Welsh speakers, and more local people frequent it than ever they did in its days of high society.

In some ways, I think, Portmeirion's contemporary fulfilment is a fulfilment of prophecy. Clough did have vatic powers! His slightly surreal effrontery is more suited to the 21st century than it was to the 20th. His environmental message is much more relevant. The sensation is even more magical nowadays, when Portmeirion's daytime crowds of high summer give way at dusk to the profound sense of peace that is indigenous to the peninsula.

And grand old Clough himself seems to me as alive as ever – sometimes rather *too* alive! – in Portmeirion's vivid sense of self-satisfaction. If you do come across his curious masterpiece unawares, to see its exotic towers, domes and pinnacles rising so improbably from the Welsh foreshore, it will still astonish you, puzzle you, perhaps make you scoff, even antagonize you; but it will almost certainly make you smile by the sheer unlikely presence of it, and by the idiosyncratic spirit of delight that Clough Williams-Ellis imagined into it long ago.

I have a dreaded vision of mechanized man in a macadamised desert – CLOUGH WILLIAMS-ELLIS, 1970

PORTMEIRION AND ITS CREATOR
Alwyn W Turner

OPPOSITE: The Dome and Colonnade with, in the foreground, a pair of Ionic pillars surmounted by gilded Burmese dancers.

ABOVE RIGHT: Portrait of Clough in oil by Oswald Birley (1926). This was presented to Clough in part-payment for designing a studio for Birley.

Portmeirion, wrote *The Times* in 1973, is 'the last folly of the Western World.' The same piece went on to say of the man who created the village: 'Would any novelist have dared to invent someone like Clough Williams-Ellis, who transforms his estate on the Welsh coast into an Italianate fantasy, a kind of stage-set of the imagination?'

At the time, the newly knighted Sir Clough had just celebrated his 90th birthday and, clad in his trademark knee-breeches, foppish waistcoat and yellow stockings, certainly cut an implausible figure in a Britain dominated by strikes, power-cuts and an incipient three-day week. The oldest practising architect in the country, the prophet of environmentalism (before such a word even existed) and the veteran of a hundred political campaigns, he had spent his adult lifetime seeking to bring 'a taste of lavishness, gaiety and cultivated design' to a public that was often more prepared to listen than were the critics. He was undeniably eccentric – a throwback to the Edwardian era of the gentleman amateur, to the manners and courtesy of the time, and to the optimism and progressive thinking of H G Wells and Bernard Shaw – but that was far from the whole story.

ABOVE: Views of
Portmeirion by WF
Baldwin (1899-1984).
Baldwin presented
Clough with a series of
six views which he
sketched at Portmeirion
in 1959.

Because despite the eccentricities of both the man and his architecture, Portmeirion was never intended to be, and never was, simply a folly. This fabulous fairytale world, this romantic Ruritarian retreat on which he worked for half a century may have provided a refuge for writers as diverse as Noel Coward and Bertrand Russell and for royalty from Edward VIII to King Zog of Albania, may have inspired musicians like Fairport Convention and Jools Holland, may most famously have been used as the setting for the TV series *The Prisoner*, but ultimately it was a practical and pragmatic, even a didactic, enterprise, albeit one that came in disguise as the trivial pursuit of pleasure. Clough's lightness of touch has sometimes concealed the seriousness of his purpose. Portmeirion was built to demonstrate that development need not be at the expense of the environment, to inspire a love of design and – not least – to be a self-sufficient business venture. On all three counts, it has proved a triumphant success.

'If there is a regret,' commented the architectural press in the early years, 'it is in the thought that so beautiful a place could not survive. Such pleasures do not seem made to be permanent.' But they were made to be permanent, and it does survive. As he approached the end of his life, Clough could look back with a sense of satisfaction, and not a little amazement: 'It was called a mad escapade at the beginning,' he said. 'But its economic success has staggered me.' And as the 21st century dawned, Portmeirion was still attracting a quarter of a million visitors a year, having survived the Depression, the Second World War and Austerity, and thrived despite the changing patterns of recreation. The first purpose-built holiday resort in Britain – still a family-run business – shows no signs of losing its unique appeal.

RIGHT: Toll House with
its painted oak statue
of St Peter and Susan
Williams-Ellis' black
sheep cut-out.

OPPOSITE: Portmeirion in its spectacular setting on the Dwyryd Estuary opposite Ynys Gifftan with views to the mountains of Meirionnydd beyond.

'HE LOOKED RATHER PECULIAR'

Bertram Clough Williams-Ellis was born in 1883, the fourth of the six children (all boys) of the Reverend John Clough Williams-Ellis, Fellow of Sidney Sussex College, Cambridge, and Rector of Gayton, Northants. The young Clough, as he early styled himself, was born in the Rectory, but at the age of four, the family returned to its native North Wales, where – despite his establishment of a London practice in later years – he was to make his home, and which shaped much of his life.

ABOVE: Clough and his brothers yachting in 1897. From left to right: Clough, John (who was killed in the Boer War) and Eric.

For an independent minded and nonconformist child, there was much against which to rebel. His father was a mid-Victorian gentleman – 'he expected to obey and be obeyed' – whilst Clough's education at Oundle School (which 'seemed to have no time for the arts and little for the humanities') and at Trinity College, Cambridge, where he went to study the Natural History Tripos, did nothing to encourage the love of building that he had acquired at an early age. Abandoning his

OPPOSITE: Clough's preliminary designs for Llangoed Hall near Brecon for Archibald Christie, 1913. Pencil, brown pen and some black pen with watercolour (755x560mm).

ABOVE: Llangoed Hall as it now is. The Hall continues to function as one of Wales' leading country house hotels.

scientific studies, he left University without completing the course and made an abortive attempt at a career in engineering, before resolving that, despite initial family misgivings, he should at least try to become an architect.

He enrolled as a student at the Architectural Association in London, but it was to be an even briefer stay than his time at Cambridge had been. After just one term he received his first commission and, finding that classes and practice were incompatible, he left to set up in business. Years later when he met Edwin Lutyens, the designer of New Delhi and the man who Clough said 'influenced me architecturally more than did anyone else,' he mentioned that he had only three months training in the profession. 'What, you took three months?' replied the great man. 'Why, I was through with it all in three weeks!' Given their subsequent success, both men could afford to be cavalier, but Clough was well aware of the limitations of his education, as he revealed in the 1930s when the question of registration of architects came before Parliament: 'Such ignorance as mine when I first gaily called myself "architect",' he wrote, 'was a real danger to the public, and nothing but the most rare good luck in zealous contractors and saintly clients can account for my not having stumbled into early and serious disaster.'

He was being typically self-deprecating of his own aptitude and application, but he did have the social benefits of birth to give him a start: that first commission had come, he acknowledged 'through family jobbery'. For while the family was not wealthy, it was certainly comfortable and had considerable connexions and status as Anglo-Welsh gentry. Clough was now the second son – the eldest had been killed in the Boer War, the next had died in infancy – and in 1908 his father gave him his inheritance, an old family house known as Plas Brondanw in Merioneth, North Wales, that had been converted into separate dwellings for seven families, and that he spent the remainder of his life developing and improving. It was, as Clough was later to note, 'an anchor', but the more immediately useful contribution made to his career by his parentage and background was the access it allowed into polite social circles, where potential clients might be encountered.

Entering the world of London society, he gradually found work and in 1912 got what he called 'my first big job': Llangoed Hall, a 17th century house to which he was introduced when he bumped into the owner on the train back to London from a hunt ball. Retaining one wing, he created a superb mansion in the Jacobean style that was the last of the great Edwardian country houses. It was also, however, his only major project before the outbreak of the war disrupted a promising career.

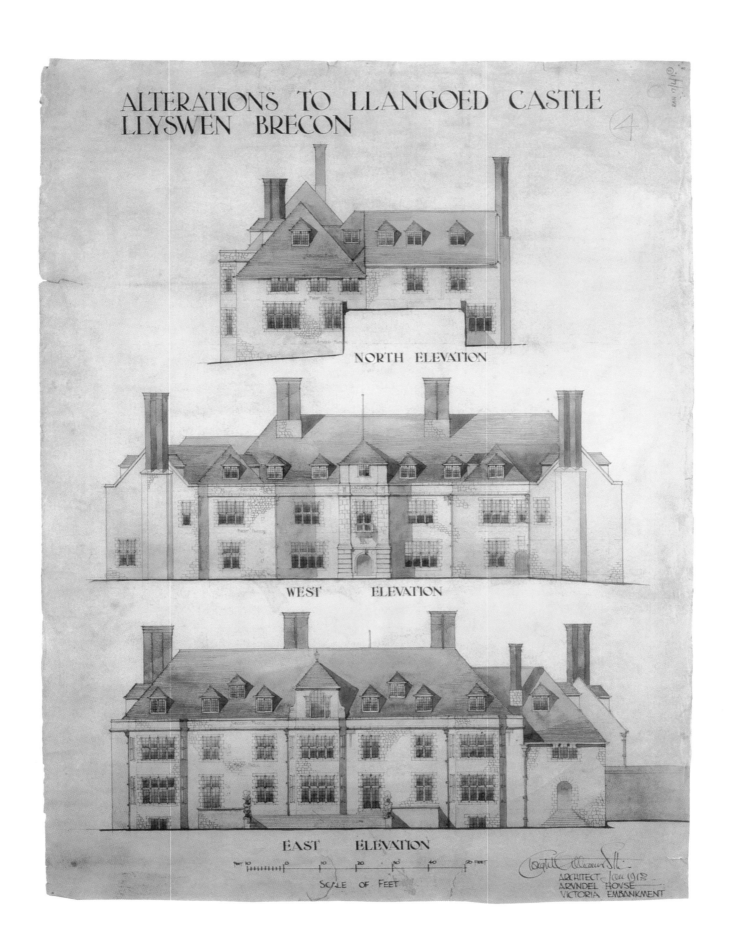

ALTERATIONS TO LLANGOED CASTLE
LLYSWEN BRECON

NORTH ELEVATION

WEST ELEVATION

EAST ELEVATION

SCALE OF FEET

ARCHITECT Jan 1913
ARVNDEL HOVSE
VICTORIA EMBANKMENT

One other event from the pre-War years was to prove of even greater significance. St Loe Strachey, the editor and proprietor of *The Spectator*, was amongst those in Edwardian society concerned at the lack of rural housing and, in an attempt to publicize the problem, he organized a competition to design a cottage that could be built for £100. Attending the launch of this initiative, Clough found his attention caught by a young woman and 'immediately resolved that I must somehow contrive to meet and see more of this girl.' She turned out to be Strachey's daughter, Amabel, and she failed to share his instant interest: 'The first time I saw him, all I thought was that he looked absurd… With his rather rakish good looks, his tall gipsy figure and one of those suspect felt hats, he looked to me rather peculiar, certainly not much like the usual run of my dancing partners.' Nonetheless, Clough entered the competition, won it (with 'a four-roomed cottage that cost precisely £101, complete'), and ultimately won the girl as well: they were married at St Martha's Chapel, Albury in July 1915.

By this stage, Clough was in uniform. He'd signed up to the Army on the declaration of war and transferred to the Welsh Guards when they were founded in 1915, subsequently serving as an intelligence officer in the Tank Corps in the last year of the conflict. Characteristically, when asked by his fellow officers what he would like for a wedding present, he asked for a ruin and, with the contributions that were donated, did indeed build a ruin of his own in the grounds

of Plas Brondanw. His dilettante pose, however, could not entirely conceal his courage: rising to the rank of Major, he was awarded the Military Cross and bar and was twice mentioned in dispatches during his service on the Western Front.

On his return from France, Clough collaborated with Amabel on his first book, *The Tank Corps*, which was considered significant enough to warrant serialization in the *Daily Telegraph*. The couple later wrote *The Pleasures of Architecture* (1924) which has rightly been described as 'one of the best introductions to the art ever written.'

Clough's main objective, though, was to pick up the strands of his pre-War career. Initially, believing that 'individualism and private interests had to a large extent been merged in a communal effort' during hostilities, and hoping that this might be extended into reconstruction, he took a job as supervising architect at the Ministry of Agriculture, but it soon became clear that the government's stated policy of building 'homes fit for heroes' was more rhetoric than reality, and he left to return to private practice, with ever greater success. His clients again came from those members of the upper echelons of society who were eager to have country houses built or restored and who, despite his 'mildly leftist views', were predominantly such leading Tories as Edward Carson and Andrew Bonar Law, though he also converted a manor house for Oswald Mosley, then still a Labour MP (and indeed his brother-in-law's best man). His most notable political client,

ABOVE: The 'ruin' built in the grounds of Plas Brondanw as a wedding present from Clough's fellow officers.

however, was the former Liberal prime minister, David Lloyd George, whose grave he was to design in later years.

Interspersed with these predominantly domestic buildings were such major projects as the First Church of Christ Scientist in Belfast, the first purpose-built Youth Hostel at Maeshafn, Clwyd, and the conversion of the Duke of Buckingham's old stately home into Stowe School.

Clough was, in short, a prospering and in-demand architect, a man who – at a time when the modernism of the Bauhaus school in Germany and of Le Corbusier in France was being much talked about (though seldom practised) in Britain – could be counted on by a cautious client as a safe pair of hands. But there was a greater ambition lurking, as he put it, 'in my mind, and by no means at the back of it.' Ever since he had first been attracted to architecture as a boy of primary school age, he had had a dream that one day he would 'erect a whole group of buildings on my own chosen site for my own satisfaction; an ensemble that would indeed *be* me.' The opportunity to realize that dream came in 1925.

'THE REALIZATION OF MY DREAMS'

In search of the ideal site on which to build his dream development, Clough had spent some considerable time scouting round the coastline of Britain for a suitable island. But the difficulties of the endeavour, the logistical challenge of construction as well as the access for visitors, eventually convinced him that an island was not the answer. A coastal

location, though, was clearly important for what he had in mind, if only such a place could be found. And then Providence delivered a solution: his uncle, Sir Osmond Williams, who lived at Deudraeth Castle in Merioneth, asked if he would have a look at a property he owned with a view to finding a purchaser.

The property in question was a century-old house just a few miles south of Clough's own home at Plas Brondanw. It occupied what had formerly been the site of a small village called Aber Iâ (which translated as 'Frozen Mouth' referring

ABOVE: A postcard of Aber Iâ as it existed before the First World War, and (left) the Hotel as it is today.

Clough adopted a mermaid as the symbol of Portmeirion from the outset. One of the existing buildings on the site, a gardener's bothy, was converted and renamed the Mermaid, whilst his own depiction of the subject was used as an early Portmeirion logo. This design was used on some of the earliest pottery commissioned for Portmeirion (below right) made by Ashtead Potters Ltd, set-up by Sir Lawrence Weaver to provide employment for disabled ex-servicemen between 1923 and 1935.

The most familiar mermaid image in the Village, however, came when work was being carried out on the Sailors' Home in Liverpool (above, and above right) in 1954; Clough bought a set of 30 mermaid panels, which can be seen throughout Portmeirion, including (left) on the Gazebo, designed by Susan Williams-Ellis and opened by Sir Hugh Casson in 1983 to mark the centenary of Clough's birth.

ABOVE: Images on the back of the Colonnade, designed by Bronwyn Williams-Ellis.

to a river-mouth); complete with a watermill, and possibly also a boatyard, the place had seen a not very successful attempt to mine lead, and an even less successful venture into gold-mining. As these somewhat ill-judged excursions into industry died out, the big house was built, and 'the poor little hamlet made way for lawns and terraces, fountains, rockeries, grottoes, paths and drives as the elegant setting for the new stuccoed mansion.' This, however, was not quite what Clough found when he arrived in 1925. The last tenant had died during the War, an eccentric old woman who had allowed the property to become overgrown and neglected to such an extent that a path had to be cut through to allow her body to be removed for burial. It was, he wrote, like the Palace of Sleeping Beauty. And he fell in love: 'It had all and more – much more – than I had ever dreamed of as desirable for my perfect little site – beetling cliffs and craggy pinnacles, level plateaux and little valleys, a tumbling cascade, splendid old trees and exotic flowering shrubs: a coastline of rocky headlands, caves and sandy bays.'

Leaping at this glorious opportunity, Clough purchased the house and its adjoining land for £5000, aiming to build here the village that had previously existed only in his imagination.

In his mind was Portofino in Northern Italy, the old Roman fishing-town that had enchanted him along with so many other visitors to the Italian Riviera. 'We awoke in brilliant sunshine to enchantment,' he wrote of his stay there, 'bells

RIGHT: The Gloriette, inspired by Schönbrunn near Vienna was built in 1964-65 to front the Piazza. It incorporated four Ionic columns which Clough had acquired in the 1930s but subsequently lost – they were rediscovered buried under a compost heap.

BELOW: The Colonnade, pictured shortly after its re-location to Portmeirion in 1959 with the Chantry (built in 1937) above.

ringing, the people just astir, fishing boats setting out, a pervading smell of fresh bread and delicious coffee, and a back-cloth of simple, colourful, unaffected southern building huddled all around us. How should I *not* have fallen for Portofino?' But, despite the similarities of a coastal cluster of buildings under a steep wooded backdrop, and even of the weather – for Aber Iâ enjoyed a micro-climate that allowed for exotic plantings – the idea was to draw inspiration not to re-make; it was, he pointed out, 'no sort of copy whether in grouping or detail, but an attempt to capture some of the friendly intimacy of so many old coastal towns and villages in the South and particularly Portofino.'

ABOVE LEFT: The Angel and Neptune, two of the first cottages built by Clough in 1926, photographed shortly after their erection, and (above) the entrance to the Golden Dragon Bookshop that occupies the ground floor of Neptune.

Apart from architectural considerations, the major difference was in usage. Portofino and the other Italian towns that so attracted Clough had grown organically as working villages, based for the most part on the fishing industry. His own creation was intended to serve primarily as a holiday destination, aimed – initially at least – at those who would recognize the Mediterranean references of the painted plasterwork buildings. Time would add its own patina, but at the outset this was essentially a ready-made stage-set that harked back to the Grand Tour as much as it looked forward to the age of tourism.

Work began immediately, firstly to clear the tangled undergrowth, then to convert the house into a hotel and the stable block into additional accommodation, and finally to erect the first two new buildings on the site: the cottages that were named Angel and Neptune. One further change was made prior to opening: the original name of Aber Iâ, with 'its chilly sound', was dropped for something 'both euphonious and indicative of its whereabouts, "Meirion" giving its county and "Port" placing it on the coast.'

From the very beginning Clough was clear that what he was attempting was what would now be called a sustainable environment. The development, he explained to the *Cambrian News* at the time of the opening, was to be 'as native to the soil and as much in harmony with the lovely surroundings as any villages that lie on the slopes of the Italian hills or the shores of the Riviera. My one great object will be to keep it unspoilt, to make it harmonize with, and not be a blot upon, the wonderful landscape.' And he went on to draw a comparison that was not perhaps obvious to others: 'A great deal of the scenery in Wales is – or should

OVERLEAF: The entrance to Portmeirion, through Bridge House.

ABOVE: Details from
Lady's Lodge (top) and
the Round House.

I say was – like Northern Italy in general character. In Wales, as in Italy, you suddenly come across these little hummocks of whitewashed cottages clustering around a church and in perfect harmony with the natural beauties of the district.'

Portmeirion opened its doors at Easter 1926, which that year fell on the first weekend of April, less than twelve months since Clough had acquired the site. The guest-list was a guide to his social circle of the time: his father-in-law, St Loe Strachey, of course (his own father had died in 1913), but also Lady Rhondda, a militant Suffragette who had survived the torpedoing of the *Lusitania*, the celebrated actress Dorothy Massingham, the former Liberal cabinet minister Harold Baker, and Lady Sheffield, wife of another former Liberal MP. Some thirty people in total gathered that weekend to inaugurate the new hotel and to endure a series of disasters. Virtually everything that could go wrong did go wrong: 'The water pump broke down, the electricity was cut off and the range blew up'. But, wrote Amabel later, 'the weather was radiant and Clough carried it off.'

Indeed the amateurish nature of the enterprise was part of the appeal. Within a month of Portmeirion opening, the General Strike was to shatter the complacency of middle-Britain, but for the liberal end of the political and artistic establishment, the 1920s were and remained a glorious playground, a time in which a certain level of discomfort could happily be seen as adding to the fun. And this was undoubtedly the target market of what *Country Life* referred to (in inverted commas) as the 'holiday village' of Portmeirion: initial charges for paying guests were 16 shillings a day, with baths 1 shilling extra, 3 shillings for breakfast and lunch, and 5 shillings and sixpence for dinner, which meant that a day's stay at full-board equated to around 50% of the average weekly wage for a male manual worker. Even the lack of an alcohol licence for the hotel – this being a time when the Temperance movement still held great sway in North Wales – and the initial absence of a telephone were not sufficient to deter pleasure-seekers. And once the original manager was dismissed ('because she would insist on economizing') to be replaced in 1927 by the painter and restaurateur James Wylie, who remained in the job until 1953, a certain consistency was instilled into the proceedings. The accommodation may have been Spartan by modern standards, but for an elite few the resort was an achievable adventure.

Clough himself was filled with optimism for the future. 'By the end of that first summer,' he wrote, 'I was sure that enough people felt as I did about it to justify my going right ahead in the realization of my dreams.' The first advert, placed in

ABOVE: The Hotel staff in 1926, and (above right) James Wylie, the long-serving manager of the Hotel, pictured here with his parrot, Agatha.

The Times in September 1926, trumpeted the appeal of the place: 'The old mansion has been transformed into a small FIRST-CLASS HOTEL; unique situation; famous sub-tropical gardens, wide sands, miles of private walks along indented coast with unsurpassed scenery. At its best autumn and early spring.' The start of the following season saw an unabashed appeal to those tempted by foreign climes: 'Abroad? No and Yes. But those blue mountain peaks slung around the bay, the hanging gardens fringing the sea, with palm and mimosa, the gaily colour-washed buildings on the little quay, the foreign tongue – ? Merely Welsh.'

The solitude and isolation were celebrated in intellectual circles. 'If you are engaged on a novel or a history of architecture,' commented a contemporary account, 'you can cook alone, and you will never be interrupted.' Amongst those who took up the offer were George Bernard Shaw – apparently unperturbed by Amabel's dismissive review in *The Spectator* of one of his works as being 'dull' and 'a slightly nauseous farce' – and Bertrand Russell, who wrote *Freedom and Organization 1814–1914* whilst staying in 1934. 'There have been only two days of fog throughout the winter,' the latter noted in a letter that February, 'and a very large number of days with continuous bright sunshine. I do not know any other part of the British Isles where the winter climate is so agreeable.'

The biggest social coup, however, was the visit in May 1934 of the Prince of Wales, later to become (briefly) Edward VIII. It was also the most inconvenient, necessitating the installation of a bath and WC in his room, since a shared bathroom was apparently inappropriate for royalty. Amabel, with a novelist's eye,

ABOVE RIGHT: The Hotel in the early-1930s, and (right) a group of guests taking tea on the lawn in the 1920s.

OVERLEAF: Portmeirion and the estuary in March 1939, with the Observatory Tower in the foreground. Fort Henry, a ruined folly used for bathing and picnicking can be seen in the middle distance.

ABOVE: A pass allowing admission to the Village, 1932

LEFT: The Hotel dining-room in the 1930s and (above left) two postcards of Portmeirion from the same period.

appraised him as 'a sensitive and slightly unsure young man whom fate had put in a very extraordinary situation, one only bearable to a stalwart extrovert.' Her attempts, however, to engage him in conversation about Julius Streicher's notorious magazine *Der Stürmer* (she had recently returned from a visit to Nazi Germany) were unsuccessful.

The enthusiasm with which Portmeirion had been greeted encouraged Clough to commence building in earnest, subsidizing the development from the proceeds of his more orthodox architectural work. 'Despite the economic gloom,' he later wrote, 'the season of 1931 proved that we had not gone too far or too fast, but quite embarrassingly, that we had under-estimated our growing popularity. The big brand-new curvilinear restaurant on the sea-edge, opened a little doubtfully for Easter, was, by August, hopelessly inadequate for its dual purpose of serving both residents and day-visitors.'

Between the opening of the hotel and the outbreak of war in 1939, a further fifteen structures were added: Watch House, Battery, the Bell Tower, Government House, Prior's Lodging, Toll House, Pilot House, Dolphin, Trinity, Anchor, Chantry, Fountain, the Observatory Tower, the Town Hall, Lady's Lodge. Each was designed as a unique piece though it was the relationship between them, and their positioning within the landscape, that was of over-riding importance to Clough. In later years he was to say apologetically that though he had 'an acute inborn instinct for architecture, I still remain in some respects half-baked as a technician.' Others were to agree – 'He was perhaps more properly a designer than an architect,' read one obituary – but even so there remain some moments of supreme technique displayed in this work: the Bell Tower (1928), for

RIGHT: Clough's original design for the Bell Tower, built in 1928. Brown ink print with pen, grey washes and watercolour (970x730). Believed to have been exhibited in the Royal Academy Summer Exhibition of 1931.

PORTMEIRION
BELL TOWER
HALF INCH SCALE
C WILLIAMS ELLIS
ARCHITECT
22B EBURY STREET

PLAN AT SIXTH LEVEL

PLAN AT FIFTH LEVEL

PLAN AT FOURTH LEVEL

PLAN AT THIRD LEVEL

PLAN AT SECOND LEVEL

PLAN AT GROUND LEVEL

PLAN AT FIRST LEVEL

example, with its upper windows half the size that they appear to be from the ground, is a virtuoso display of forced perspective.

During the same period he also acquired Deudraeth Castle from the estate of his now deceased uncle, Sir Osmond Williams, half-a-mile inland from Portmeirion. 'It was when I heard,' he wrote, 'that the estate's trustees were considering an offer to purchase the place as an institution for the treatment of delinquent youths of low intelligence, that I intervened and bought it in self-defence.' The castle was opened

RIGHT: The Bell Tower, as built. It was intended to draw attention to his venture and to show that architecture should be concerned with groups of buildings in the environment.

as a subsidiary hotel, one which for pet-owners had the added benefit of allowing dogs to stay (at a charge of 2 shillings and sixpence a day) – Portmeirion itself remained off-limits to dogs, save for those in the pet cemetery founded by the previous occupant. And, recognizing that his clientele was predominantly metropolitan, he also bought a country seat named Atcham House just outside Shrewsbury, renamed it the Mytton & Mermaid and opened it as a hotel to serve as staging post for Portmeirion visitors driving up from London.

As the village – perhaps hamlet is a more appropriate term at this stage – took shape, so it began to attract praise for the boldness of its vision and its unique atmosphere. In 1928 the *Architects' Journal* rejoiced in the fact that it was 'an unbelievable and enchanted place; in nothing are you reminded of a vulgar world outside,' whilst *Country Life* described it in 1930 as 'a glorious medley of Italy, Wales, a pirate's lair, Cornwall, baroque, reason and romance.' The latter publication returned in 1976 and added a note of wistful hindsight: 'Today it strikes us as a confident approach to architecture, one optimistic about the new world of 1918.' None, though, could better Clough's own analysis that drew on a parade-ground metaphor, pointing out that the buildings are stood not at attention but at ease.

Increasingly too, Portmeirion was attracting a new group of admirers, visitors who wanted to explore and enjoy but not to stay. Since a major part of Clough's purpose had been propagandist ('I was aiming at winning an as yet uninterested and uninformed popular support for architecture, planning, landscaping, the use of colour and indeed for design generally'), this was naturally to be welcomed. Yet the problem arose of how to protect the fledgling enterprise from being over-run. And the answer, Clough concluded, was to charge an admission fee, though with a characteristic quirk, he decided it should be variable, rising and falling with the waves of day visitors. A notice at the entrance read: 'In order sufficiently to discourage visitors to Portmeirion and to keep their numbers within acceptable limits, it has been found necessary in impose a toll of __. Those wishing to avoid this impost are advised to turn back here.' The normal price in the 1930s was 1 shilling, though during the Prince of Wales' stay it reached the (princely) sum of 10 shillings. The money raised was, of course, ploughed back into further building and development.

BELOW: The Town Hall during construction (1937-38).

ABOVE: Uriah Lovell, seen here weaving a basket.

ABOVE RIGHT: The Hotel staff on the *Amis Réunis* in the 1950s.

One guest who escaped any such charges was Uriah Lovell, a basket weaver who lived in a tepee in the woods and was for some years the resident hermit on the estate (every folly needs a hermit). Commonly known as Gypsy Lovell, he was, it appears, a genuine Rom – certainly he was able to converse freely with Augustus John in Romany, as well as in English and Welsh – and was popular with visitors and proprietor alike, attracting an audience keen to hear his words of wisdom. 'Uriah is so almost always right,' wrote Clough, 'that even when (rarely) he proves wrong about the coming weather, I have a feeling that it is not he who has made the mistake.' Tragically, in January 1938, he was knocked down by a motorbike and, though he survived for a few years, he had sustained a fracture of the skull that was ultimately to cause his death.

'At present,' wrote Clough in 1931, 'it is essentially a holiday place and a seasonal one at that, but I shall not be content until I have somehow contrived that an adequate population inhabits Portmeirion as its permanent home.' He acknowledged that there was currently no serious industry ('unless one counts the painting of pictures and the writing of books'), but spoke of his desire to establish a boat-building yard and a joiner's shop. The latter did indeed materialize, as did an upholstery workshop to service the hotel, but the boat-building was hampered by the location on a tidal estuary, and the proposal of permanent residents never came to anything. Even with this dream unrealised, however, Clough could afford to look back, as the war-clouds gathered again over Europe, at a venture that could hardly have been more spectacular. Despite misgivings on the part of everyone, even from Amabel, he had turned himself into a hotelier of national and international repute.

RIGHT: The *Amis Réunis* seen from a room in the Hotel in the late-1920s.

LEFT: The Gloriette, with
Unicorn in the distance.

'MORE FUN FOR MORE PEOPLE'

Clough's obituary in *The Times* remarked that he would
'probably be remembered longest not for his country houses,
nor even for his celebrated folly-village of Portmeirion in Wales,
but for his life-long championship of the conservationist cause.'
If this is overstating the case, it is at least a reminder that there
was always a strongly educational element to his life and work,
nowhere more so than at Portmeirion.

The central theme to which he returned again and
again through his life was the need for rational,
imaginative planned development. As far back as the First
World War, while on leave from France, he had written to
the *Manchester Guardian* (as was), expounding his view
that: 'Anyone who cares for England must be interested
in national planning, the provision of a comprehensive

ABOVE: Clough in the
early-1970s.

ABOVE: A decorative
cast metal plaque inset
into a wall of the Angel
cottage.

ABOVE RIGHT: The
painted pine figurehead
from the petrol pump
installed outside
Neptune in 1926.

co-ordinated and compulsory development and conservation scheme for the country as a whole, urban and rural, public and private.' It was an argument that was to dominate much of his proselytising over the decades. 'What is the use of all this planning?' he was once asked. 'What do you expect from it?' And his answer was both indicative of his own philosophy and a gentle reminder of what is so often forgotten when the subject is considered: 'More fun for more people.'

The concern over planning derives initially from the fact that Britain was the first nation to undergo the Industrial Revolution in the late 18th century. The anarchy that ensued, in which land could be used in whatever manner its owner saw fit, bequeathed us the dark, Satanic mills lambasted by Blake and the slums that formed the backdrop to Dickens' writing. The idea that society had a right to shape a public policy towards development was anathema to the newly emergent capitalist class, and the struggle to assert control – both over standards of housing and over land use: to separate, for example, heavy industry from residential areas – took more than a century to complete. Early legislation such as the Public Health Act of 1848 and the Housing of the Working Class Act in 1890 began to address the issues of slum housing, but it was not until 1909 that the first Town Planning Act was passed, establishing that local authorities had a role to play in this field. The powers granted to councils were, however, of a very limited, discretionary nature, and by the end of hostilities in 1918, the situation remained very much a free-for-all.

OVERLEAF: The Piazza, with (from left to right) Salutation, the Gloriette and Telford's Tower.

In the aftermath of the War, hopes were high that a new Britain could be brought into being. It was the dashing of those hopes, the gradual realization that nothing had really changed, that spurred Clough into a new, more aggressively campaigning position, and that continued the politicisation begun by, as he later wrote, 'a destruction that I not only witnessed but assisted in. It was all hateful to me, and the monstrous waste and cruelty of those years still frightens me even in retrospect.' Before the War, he was by his own account, 'too timorous a nonconformist to defy convention where it seemed overwhelmingly against me.' By the mid-'20s no such reticence was evident.

His first great expression of discontent was 'a gloomy and rather angry book', *England and the Octopus*, published in 1928. On its reprint in 1975, he wrote a new

BELOW: Chantry Cottage (built 1937) and Chantry Row (built 1962-63) with Clough's half-round Onion Dome used to hide a chimney.

BELOW: Lady's Lodge
(built 1938-39),
originally a garage now
used as a shop and,
to the left, the entrance
to the Round House
(built 1959-60),
which houses the
Prisoner shop.

preface that made his feelings even more explicit: 'This is an angry book, written by an angry young man nearly half a century ago. Now I am in my ninety-second year and still angry.' In carefully weighted sentences, he spelled out his disillusion: 'In the late war we were invited to fight to preserve England. We believed, we fought. It may be well to preserve England, but better to have an England worth preserving. We saved the country, that we might ourselves destroy it.'

Though inevitably now dated in parts, *England and the Octopus* remains a fine piece of work, a fierce attack on the soulless disfigurement of the country he loved. He demanded an end to ribbon development (the then-prevalent practice of building on arterial roads without consciousness of community) and its

ABOVE: Sign on the Angel, which pre-dated the building and which gave it its name.

replacement by properly planned new towns; he called for the establishment of national parks to preserve areas of outstanding natural beauty; he proposed the burial of power lines, the statutory listing of great buildings, the control of intrusive advertising. Much of this was ultimately to be achieved (with, for example, the Ribbon Development Act of 1935), but even where it was not, he was still right, as in his contempt for the 'ill-mannered, un-neighbourly and filthy' practice of littering. In fact, even when his arguments were askew, his conclusions could have profitably have been followed, such as his criticism – purely on aesthetic grounds – of the use of asbestos: 'If you must use asbestos (*must* you?), avoid the livid pink sort as you would the scarlet fever.' And surely this book must have been the first time that many in Britain had come across the concept of Feng Shui.

The floodgates now being opened, a torrent of campaigning poured forth. 'He was,' wrote Amabel of this period, 'an extrovert, a gregarious, amusing, stimulating fellow; a hard, sly, hitter; bold to risk an action for libel, skilful with publicity, and expert at making cruel fun of the pompous and the insensitive, and not caring whom he annoyed.' And it was that combination of relentless good humour and devastatingly incisive analysis that made him such a formidable figure in public life between the Wars.

He wrote and spoke incessantly, addressing the British Health Resorts Association on 'Town Planning at the Seaside', the Eisteddfod on 'The Face of Wales', and the Anti-Noise League on the need to sound-proof housing and on the way that noise was used as a military weapon. He made his first broadcast on the

ABOVE: Amabel and John Strachey, photographed in 1910, when they were respectively 16- and 6-years-old.

wireless in 1928, a talk entitled 'Who Cares? An Architect's Grumble about the Disfigurement of England', and became a familiar voice on the airwaves, speaking on such diverse subjects as 'London Scenes', 'The Ideal Holiday' and 'Roads Uglification'. And in between he managed to fit in a bewildering range of interests from the cutting down of yew trees in Welsh churchyards to a lecture on Russia given at the Architectural Association.

Running through it all was his much-used saying that could have served as a slogan both for the principle of town planning and for environmentalism: 'There can be no private right to do a public wrong.'

In all this he had most willing encouragement and support from Amabel, who was by now making her own name as a writer. Indeed she was by far the more obviously radical of the two. 'I belonged to a political family,' she wrote, which understated the case a little. Her father, St Loe Strachey, had originally been a Liberal, but when that party split in 1886 over the issue of Ireland, he had joined the newly formed Liberal Unionists, and ultimately drifted into the ranks of the Conservative Party. His editorship of *The Spectator*, however, demonstrated that he was no party hack: he may have inclined to the right of the political spectrum on many issues, but he retained a fierce and cherished independence of thought. The attitude, if not the politics, was passed on to his children, particularly to Amabel and her younger brother, John Strachey. John's move leftwards, through the Independent Labour Party to communism, encouraged her own increasingly radical politics and, like him, she was later proud to call herself a 'class traitor'.

RIGHT: A peacock parades past Neptune down towards the Hotel.

Her first visit to the Soviet Union in 1928, in the company of John (then editor of the ILP journal *The Miner*), was followed in 1931 by a trip with her husband, on which occasion Clough was offered a job: 'and a tempting job it was – the selection of sites for, and outline planning of, New Towns for the Soviet Union, with my own train that would run me and my surveying and drawing-staff wherever required about the map of Russia.' For various reasons, including his commitment to Portmeirion, he turned down the offer to become Stalin's town planner, a decision that was probably for the best; however longingly he looked at the centralized power of autocracies, he was never a committee man and was temperamentally unsuited to the bureaucracy of the USSR. Whatever inducements were proffered, the reality could never have matched the control he exercised in Portmeirion.

ABOVE: Amabel and
Clough (both pictured
in 1937)

In the mid-1930s, with Italy, Germany, Portugal and now Spain falling to
fascism, Amabel became one of the three founding editors of *Left Review*, a radical
cultural journal, and a prominent figure in the anti-fascist movement of the period,
writing a series of political novels and leading the British Section of the
International Association of Writers for the Defence of Culture. If such activities
seem a little remote now, she pointed out in her autobiography that this was a time
when Hermann Goering was proudly boasting that, 'When I hear the word
"culture", I reach for my revolver.' For any kind of artist – let alone a writer as
gifted and committed as Amabel – these were desperate years, when civilization
itself was under threat, and when Britain was inexorably heading towards a
confrontation with fascism. Her brother was named on a German list of political
enemies to be eliminated should the Nazis ever invade, and in 1939 both he and
she had suicide pills prepared in case of such an eventuality.

Clough, on the other hand, was less overtly partisan in his politics. Amabel
herself provided the most accurate summary when she wrote that 'Clough's
conscience was mainly visual.' Even so, such was the politically charged mood of
the times, that he could hardly remain impervious to it. That first trip to Russia
had resulted in a spirited defence of what was being achieved in development
terms, given the appalling legacy of the Czarist regime, and he continued to
support the endeavours of his Soviet counterparts. A second visit, however, to
attend a 1937 architectural conference – an occasion where he met Frank Lloyd

ABOVE: Three views of Portmeirion by Meryl Watts (1910-92). Having studied at Blackheath School of Art, Watts was evacuated to North Wales at the start of the Second World War and produced woodcuts and postcards of Portmeirion.

Wright for the first time – left him troubled by the triumphal classicism of more recent building: 'The nation that has adapted, developed and worked a new political system with such stupendous results,' he wrote, 'should be able, I feel, to find also a new expression of its genius in the arts, achieve some new synthesis and a truly socialist architecture.'

Much as Clough admired the construction achievements of the Soviet Union, though, and that state's ability to give hitherto undreamt-of powers to planners, he never fell into the trap of believing that its example could be copied in Britain: such dictatorial authority might be suitable for 'opening up sparsely inhabited places' but would be 'highly undemocratic here.' Nonetheless, he and Amabel were clearly amused by the way in which, after years crying out in the wilderness, they found themselves suddenly much sought after when Russia entered the war against Germany and turned overnight from international bogeyman to much valued ally: 'We suddenly find ourselves addressing large and influential audiences on the achievements of the Soviet Union,' they wrote in 1942. 'His Worship the Mayor is in the chair, the leaders of local society are on the platform, where the grand piano, presently to accompany both "God Save the King" and the "Internationale," is prophetically draped with the Union Jack and the Red Flag, sociably entwined.'

By this stage, of course, the horrors of world war that Clough had suffered on the last occasion had returned. But still, he insisted, lessons must be learnt and somehow the disillusionment of the 1920s must be avoided. Speaking at

Cambridge University in 1938 he had issued a pre-emptive statement of intent: 'Personally he would rather be found dead among noble ruins than among mean ones,' he was reported as saying; and 'while they were alive, at least they could build something worth defending.' As a declaration of why it was worth fighting for one's beliefs, it sounded a defiant note, and towards the end of his life, he made it clear that this was still where he stood: 'Even if things did come to the worst I would still prefer to perish in a flowery dell than in some foul and noisome ditch.'

BELOW: Bridge House and Toll House. The latter was once the first point of arrival, hence the striped toll-bar and blue bell that can still be seen on the side of the building.

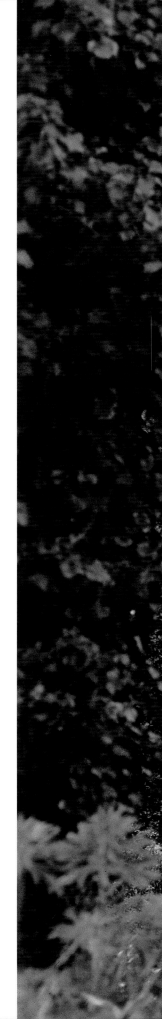

RIGHT: View from Mermaid showing Angel and the Town Hall. The astrolabe is dedicated to William Willett who introduced Summer time.

'OUR TOWNS MUST BE RE-MADE'

The German invasion of Poland on 1 September 1939 triggered the largest mass movement of people in Britain's history, as millions of children were evacuated from cities believed to be at risk from bombing and re-located to safer areas. The hotel at Deudraeth Castle was taken over by a prep school, while Clough's home at Plas Brondanw accommodated several evacuee children. By the end of the first week of September he was writing to the newspapers, already looking ahead: 'I and my neighbours are already the willing hosts of some thousands of children and their teachers evacuated from less happily situated areas. There is also, naturally, a great influx of family parties and of elderly persons, and if the war persists it must be expected that so safe and quiet an area would be particularly sought after for the establishment of convalescent hospitals and as a place for the spending of leave from the fighting fronts or from war work in the "exposed" areas.'

Portmeirion was indeed at one point requisitioned by the RAF, who intended to use it as a rest centre for airmen, but the proposal was never realized, and those servicemen who did spend time at the village (men including Guy Gibson of Dam Busters fame) did so on their own initiative. There was, however, plenty of evidence that the country was now at war. For a period, the North Welsh coast was considered a possible location for invasion, and troops were posted to Portmeirion as a precautionary measure. Anti-tank blocks were even placed on the road leading up from the hotel, until it was pointed out to the officer responsible that the measure also prevented supplies being brought in – once he understood that this included beer deliveries, the obstacles were promptly removed. Also stationed on the peninsula for a while was a brigade of Indian Mounted Artillery, engaged in mountain exercises.

ABOVE: A gilt metal sign featuring Hercules which hangs from the Town Hall.

Despite these necessary intrusions, Portmeirion remained open for business throughout the war years and, to an extent, trade remained brisk. With the Continent now out of the question as a holiday destination, the village became an even more attractive proposition for some. Most famously, it was where Noel Coward came to escape the Blitz for a week in 1941: 'I have got to write a comedy,' he told his friend Joyce Carey, 'people *must* laugh, I have got an idea and I must get on with it as soon as possible.' In the peace of Portmeirion, staying at Fountain, he had the completed manuscript of *Blithe Spirit* finished in five days, and it was on the London stage within weeks, where it set a record for a West End comedy with a run of nearly two thousand performances.

ABOVE: View looking up to (from left to right) the Dolphin, Government House and the Bell Tower, with the single-story Watch House below.

What did change was the traditional winter building programme; construction for anything but essential war work was, of course, prohibited and nothing was to be added to the village for many years. But Clough's other activities continued unabated: he was still broadcasting, still writing and still lecturing. In this latter capacity, he often found himself now addressing Army audiences, participating in the massive programme of education initiated by the Adjutant-General Sir Ronald Adam: 'The soldier who understands the cause for which he fights,' Adam had declared, 'is likely to be a more reliable soldier than the one who doesn't.' For Clough this was a most welcome development, and his contribution – along with those of thousands of others – did much to promise that peace, when finally it came, would this time produce a more progressive society than had the aftermath of 1918.

Amongst the subjects to which he turned his mind in the early years of the war was the opportunity opened up by the bombing of British cities by the Luftwaffe. He lamented, for example, the destruction of Christopher Wren's churches in London, but argued that many of those now lost had already been considered 'redundant' by the Church, and he proposed that the sites now vacated should be developed for commercial purposes, with some of the profit being used to reconstruct the churches in other parts of the country. 'There could be few towns where the authentic Phoenix-Wren church would not be the most gracious, notable and revered building in the place,' he wrote. 'If the enemy's bombs serve to disperse this cultural heritage more widely and more effectively over our country at large, there will at least be a credit side to the account.'

LEFT: Lady's Lodge (1939, left) and the Round House (1959, right). Their construction was separated by the Second World War. A bridge now joins them together.

When he was challenged over what seemed like callousness in seeing a positive side to the violence – was all this, he was asked, worth the life of a single child? – he responded with renewed fervour: 'It is largely for the sake of our children, indeed, that our towns *must* be re-made; to lower the general infant mortality rate, to increase the child's expectation of life itself as well as of happiness and of positive and resilient health. We must reduce the cruel toll of road accidents by better street planning and by providing ample playgrounds. Smoke and respiratory diseases must be banished together, along with the infectious diseases that go with dirt, darkness and overcrowding.' The insistence on looking to the future was notable. This was written in 1941, a year that saw the Blitz still in full ferocity, but also the year that saw Britain's worst-ever casualty figures for road accidents, with over 9000 killed; Clough was one of the few to recognize that the latter was likely to be a longer lasting problem than the bombing.

Asked whether the money existed for the kind of rebuilding programme that he proposed, he retorted that the war was costing fifteen million pounds a day; 'Yet there were ways in which, as I believe, the wise spending of 15 millions *a year* might not only have averted war altogether, but have made us appreciably less unlike what we profess to be – a just, democratic and civilized people.'

The suggestion of indifference to the suffering caused by war was, of course, misplaced when directed at a veteran of the Western Front. But an even more terrible reminder of the tragic waste of life was yet to come. Clough and Amabel's only son, Christopher, joined up and served in Clough's old regiment, the Welsh Guards: he was killed during the protracted struggle to capture Monte Cassino in 1944.

TOP: The Copper Boat embellishes a section of balustrade in front of the Hotel.

ABOVE: A stone figure of Nelson, given to Clough by Sir Michael Duff, and placed at the foot of the Observatory Tower.

'RETURNING SANITY'

One issue had been a regular theme in Clough's campaigning for years. As a leading member of both the Council for the Preservation of Rural England and the Council for the Protection of Rural Wales, he had been in the forefront of those lobbying for the creation of national parks, areas of such outstanding beauty that they should be made available to all, and exempted from enclosure or private development. The concept had been accepted in the USA, Canada, Australia and New Zealand back in the 19th century, but, despite the recommendations of a government committee under Lord Addison in 1931, the political will to institute such a scheme was evidently lacking in Britain.

In a commendable outburst of impatience, Clough decided to take unilateral action. In 1935 he announced that he had bought 300 acres of wild upland in his beloved Snowdonia and was donating it to the nation as the nucleus of what he hoped would become a National Park. He argued that tourism and its accompanying developments posed the threat of killing the very attraction on which it relied, and cited his own experience at Portmeirion as his credentials. 'Whereas formerly he might have been regarded as an idealist only,' it was reported, 'he had been able to develop his holdings without spoiling the countryside and to show that architectural good manners were also good business. He had proved that it was possible, by careful and sympathetic building, to exploit a place without ruining it.' His action re-ignited debate on the subject – a leader in *The Times* congratulated him on proving the adage that 'if you want a thing done, you must do it yourself' – but again the politicians procrastinated and the pressure died down.

For Clough, however, this was an issue that went to the heart of human existence and he was not prepared to let it lie: 'Man cannot survive in full bodily health and spiritual vigour if denied the healing contact with unmanipulated Nature that the wild places of our teeming country can still afford,' he argued in a 1939 article attacking the failure to implement the Addison Report.

Finally, in 1945, William Morrison, the Conservative minister of town and country planning, set up another committee, this one intended to identify what areas should be designated as national parks and how they should be run. Clough was named as a member of the committee, under the chairmanship of Sir Arthur Hobhouse, and helped ensure that this time the opportunity was not missed, even

outlining his proposed boundary for Snowdonia to George VI and Queen Elizabeth on their 1946 trip to North Wales.

By the time the committee produced its report, in 1947, the political landscape had been transformed. Even while the war with Japan continued, the electorate had removed Winston Churchill as prime minister and replaced him by the Labour government of Clement Attlee; perhaps the most radical and reforming administration in British history it was, alongside its leaps forward in health, education and industry, also to demonstrate a genuine commitment to planning issues. The new minister for town and country planning was Lewis Silkin, who had already initiated the green belt policy whilst a member of the London County Council, and who now steered through Parliament the National Parks and Access to the Countryside Act in 1949, establishing the first ten areas – including Snowdonia – to be protected. It was, Silkin proclaimed, 'the most exciting Act of the post-war Parliament,' and although Clough was disappointed by some aspects of the legislation, particularly in regard to funding, he was quick to pay tribute to the man responsible: 'With all its blemishes and vices it is something that we might not have had at all but for the Minister's own resolve.'

It was Silkin too who brought in the Town & Country Planning Act in 1947, a massive Bill that began by wiping the slate clean and repealing all previous legislation in the field, before setting out a new standard. Henceforth all development was to be subject to statutory local authority control, with councils charged with producing local development plans. And, for the first time, buildings of architectural or historical interest were to be listed and preserved for the nation. Clough, who – as a member of the Society for the Protection of Ancient Buildings – had denounced an earlier Act and called for 'reality in place of an ineffectual gesture,' was much heartened: at the end of his life he was still citing the 1947 Act as 'an encouraging sign of returning sanity.'

These landmark pieces of legislation are not as celebrated as they might be, perhaps because Silkin himself was a less than charismatic figure in a government of giants (including John Strachey as Minister for Food), and was without a union or party power-base to promote his profile. But they set out the groundwork of much that was to be achieved; without the introduction of compulsory purchase,

BELOW: Clough's conservation: a path in the Gwyllt with Rhododendron facetum.

LEFT: The Bell Tower with Battery and Prior's Lodging in the foreground and Government House in the background.

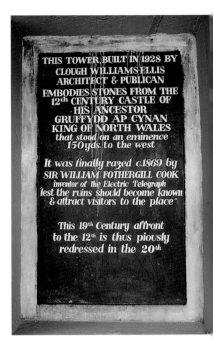

for example, the much-trumpeted schools and hospitals, let alone the council housing, would never have been built. And Silkin himself had no doubt that these were genuinely socialist measures; without the National Parks Act, he declared, the people of Britain 'are fettered, deprived of their powers of access and facilities needed to make holidays enjoyable. With it the countryside is theirs to preserve, to cherish, to enjoy, to make their own.'

He had one other measure that was to change the lives of countless thousands, and again it was something that Clough had been agitating for over many years. The New Towns Act of 1946 designated fourteen areas in Britain, mostly in the South-East, that were to be developed as new urban centres to soak up the population of the cities. The first of these was Stevenage, and Clough was appointed the first chairman of the Advisory Council.

Where the other Acts introduced by Silkin had primarily met with criticism for not going far enough, this was a much more controversial proposal. However much he claimed that 'People from all over the world will come to Stevenage to see how we here in this country are building for the new way of life,' the opposition was vociferous and sustained. Amongst those most distraught by the proposal was E M Forster, whose novel *Howard's End* had been based on a house in Stevenage that was now to be swallowed up in the new conurbation. Forster took Clough to meet the residents of this house, which proved to be a scarring experience: 'Never in all my life,' wrote Clough, 'have I been received with such implacable hostility.' But his argument was sound enough: 'It was inevitable that some old inhabitants would be disturbed, some even dispossessed, but if a hitherto fortunate fifty had now to give up something for a long-deprived fifty thousand, was there anything very wicked about that?'

His time at Stevenage was brief, lasting under a year, before he realized that he was 'highly allergic to committees and paper-work generally' and resigned, or – as he put it – Silkin 'very kindly sacked me.' The experience was, he wrote, 'an exhilarating prospect too soon clouded over by unforeseen national economic crises and my own basic unfitness for *administration*, as against actual planning and building ploys.'

The democratic impulse, however, which ultimately derived – in however roundabout a fashion – from his concern with planning, was to stand him in good stead. And it had one further manifestation, unexpected from a figure so often considered somewhat patrician in outlook, in those immediate post-War years. If Portmeirion was the first purpose-built holiday resort in Britain, it was by no means the last. At Easter 1936, ten years on from Portmeirion's launch, Billy

TOP: The plaque at the base of the Bell Tower, apologizing on behalf of the 20th century for the demolition of the 12th century castle built by Clough's ancestors.

ABOVE: A Wyvern by the sea steps near the Hotel.

ABOVE: A view of Portmeirion by Meryl Watts. One of many designs sold as postcards in Portmeirion after the Second World War.

RIGHT: Unicorn in snow.

Butlin had opened his first holiday camp in Skegness. It had been followed in 1938 by another in Clacton, though the onward march was soon halted by hostilities.

Amongst the sites that Butlin had acquired by this stage was one at Pwllheli in Caernarfonshire, which the Admiralty requisitioned in 1940 for use as a military training camp, promising him its return once the War was over. But, come peacetime, the local authority attempted to move the goalposts and objected to the development of the resort. Clough was already on record as a defender of the 'big holiday camps,' pointing out they were far too new to be judged by how they currently appeared. Now he was called upon to appear at the planning inquiry, and he upset many by his evidence in favour of the project. 'Are we already forgetting,' he argued, 'that throughout the long years of war most of our countrymen and women have been at full stretch and virtually without holidays at all?' Pwllheli may not have been his preferred choice of location, 'but there it is and there I say it should remain if the greatest happiness of the greatest number means a thing to us.'

He spoke as a man who had again been inspired by the way the nation had come together in times of adversity (such class collaboration 'might even make the primitive and un-English expedient of the firing squad unnecessary,' he remarked), and he spoke as a man who knew that times were changing, in many ways for the better.

'WE WENT TO PORTMEIRION'

ABOVE AND ABOVE RIGHT:
Two Meryl Watts
postcard designs for
Portmeirion.

'Not the least of Clough's delights at Portmeirion,' wrote Amabel, 'was not having a client. He could be the sole arbiter, for there were also, then, no Building Regulations, no Town & Country Planning Act, no regulations about Historic Buildings and, though he thought there ought to be all these things (and he said so repeatedly), privately, secretly, he relished their absence.' He put it somewhat more obliquely himself – 'I must call my own tune, so I alone must pay the piper' – but the point remained: here, removed from the everyday world of the construction industry, he was in the enviable position of being designer, client and developer, virtually a law unto himself. He even ensured that the boundaries of the Snowdonia National Park avoided Portmeirion.

In the immediate post-War period, however, there was no building to be done. Shortages of materials and labour, and the urgent need to re-build a ravaged nation, meant non-essential, private construction work was simply banned; it was not until 1954 that the first new structure (Gate House) was finished, starting a second phase of building that was to last fifteen years and that effectively completed the village.

RIGHT: The entrance
to Portmeirion, via
Gate House.

OVERLEAF: View towards
the Town Hall with the
statue of Hercules
flanked by the
Bandstand and Angel.

ABOVE: An oval grille that came from the Old Bank of England and is now in the Town Hall.

ABOVE RIGHT: A corbel of Clough's head carved by Jonah Jones to replace a missing original on the Bristol Colonnade.

The length of time that Portmeirion took to complete helped to ensure that what might have been in different circumstances, and different hands, a uniform concept has instead acquired an organic feel. 'Because I like experimenting – in materials as well as in shapes and colours,' wrote Clough, 'the buildings are certainly a pretty mixed lot and their several dates from 1926 onwards have been reflected in their appearance.' It was an effect that was, in part, consciously created, with buildings painted in stages and in differing shades to convey the sense of being weathered, but some of it was simply that Clough's attention had fallen upon a novel concept that he wished to explore. The Pantheon (1961), for example, whose dome dominates the entry into Portmeirion, suggests a religious function, but actually arose because he felt the village suffered from the hitherto unknown condition of 'dome deficiency.' As he acknowledged, he had no idea what is was actually *for* ('which is naturally shocking to serious-minded people'), but simply felt that it would sit well in the landscape.

Similarly, he had a notion that arches would make the entrance more dramatic, delaying the revelation of the wonders beyond, so Gate House (1955) and Bridge House (1971) were constructed. Other structures appeared equally self-indulgent but actually had a more definite purpose, notably the Band Stand (1961), which conceals an electrical substation.

Further diversity of development came with the importing of other architects' works. Just before the War, Clough had introduced a new element when he discovered that Emral Hall in Flintshire was scheduled for demolition and sale. Having failed to convince anyone else that it should be preserved, he attended the auction himself and bought the barrel-vaulted ceiling to the ballroom, on which was depicted the labours of Hercules; then, needing an appropriate setting for his new piece, he bought the rest of the room and some more of the building as well. All of it was carefully taken apart and transported to Portmeirion, where it was re-assembled to become the Town Hall.

His imagination thus fired, he announced that an additional function of the village would be as 'a home for fallen buildings'. Most spectacular of all was the colonnade of the 18th century Bath House at Arnos Court, Bristol, which he acquired in 1957 and re-erected in an extraordinary labour of love. Nor was it the

LEFT: Hercules by
William Brodie (1815-
1881), cast around
1863 and bought by
Clough in Edinburgh in
1960. The plinth carries
plaques by Jonah
Jones commemorating
various fine summers.

only structure that caught his eye; in 1959 it was revealed that the triumphal arch at Paganhill, which had been built in 1834 to commemorate the abolition of slavery, was due to be demolished by Stroud Council. If necessary, Clough wrote, 'I would myself gladly subscribe half of whatever proved the cost of careful taking down, and the transport to and re-erection at Portmeirion, North Wales, where, at the head of a long, wide, formal flight of steps leading down to the sea, it could be done appropriate honour, and where it would have the company of other distinguished but slighted monuments similarly translated.' In the event, Stroud Council relented and the arch remained in its original home, but Clough found an alternative feature for the location with the statue of Hercules, originally cast in the 1860s by William Brodie, creator most famously of the memorial to Greyfriars Bobby in Edinburgh.

The resumption of this building work after the years of austerity may have suggested a return to normality, but in fact the country – and its use of leisure-time – had changed markedly, as the dispute over the Pwllheli Butlin's indicated. The 1947 film *Holiday Camp* (the movie that introduced Jack Warner and Kathleen Harrison as the Huggetts) depicted a new world, in which the working-class were demanding more than a no-frills B&B in Clacton, and instead heading for the comforts of the designed resort. Cecil Day-Lewis had described the pre-War version of such a camp in his 1940 crime novel *Malice in Wonderland*: 'The luxuriant Sleepeesi mattress wooing the tired reveller into the arms of Morpheus, the water (H. and C.), the electric light, hanging wardrobe and 100% damp-proof walls ... Luxury indeed.' All for £3 10s a week, 'inclusive of everything.' The Mass Observer who is the hero of the book worries that such conditions may lead the happy campers to question the very structure of society: 'Is the luxury of this place likely to dissatisfy you with your normal home and work environment?' he asks them. 'Does it create envy of those who can afford such food, recreation etc all the year round? Or do you accept such differences of income as in the nature of things?'

Clough was not immune to the growing demands for comfort on the part of holiday-makers – as long ago as 1934 he had argued for en-suite bathrooms and proper sound insulation, and condemned bad lighting, the 'mistaking of display for comfort, and thinking insufficiently of the staff's comfort.' Now, in addition to the new structures came a spate of improvements to the existing buildings: 'kitchens, drains, electricity supplies, all had to be renewed or replaced, and twenty or thirty private bathrooms added.' The 'relatively restricted patronage of the well-to-do

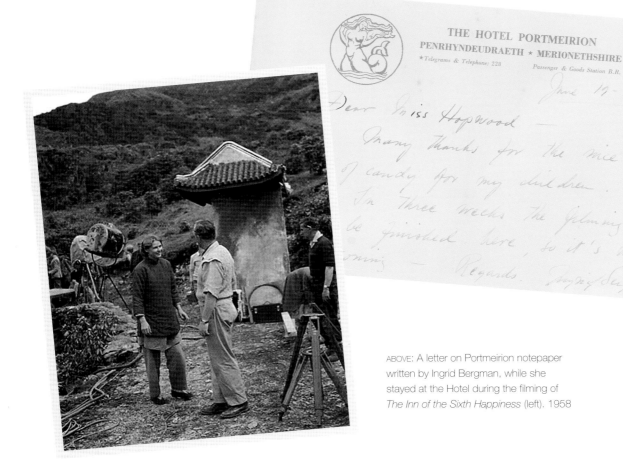

THE HOTEL PORTMEIRION
PENRHYNDEUDRAETH ★ MERIONETHSHIRE
★ Telegrams & Telephone: 228   Passenger & Goods Station B.R.

June 19-58

Dear Miss Hopwood —
Many thanks for the nice
candy for my children.
In three weeks the filming
be finished here, so it's no
coming — Regards, Ingrid Bergman

ABOVE: A letter on Portmeirion notepaper
written by Ingrid Bergman, while she
stayed at the Hotel during the filming of
The Inn of the Sixth Happiness (left). 1958

intelligentsia' on which Portmeirion had relied pre-War, the
class to which Clough and Amabel themselves belonged, was
no longer sufficient to sustain the resort. They still came, of
course – Charles Laughton, an old friend to whom they had
been introduced by H G Wells, stayed during his last great
year in the theatre, the 1959 season at Stratford when he
played King Lear, while John Osborne wrote his play *Luther*
here in 1961 and Joseph Needham, the great biochemist and
historian of China, was a regular visitor – but they were no
longer the only ones seeking admission. There was now a
new wave of day visitors, typified perhaps by Vera McLean of
Cheadle writing a postcard to her aunt in 1956: 'We went to
Portmeirion – it is the place where the film stars go – it is
like a little village – you have to pay to look round.' And in
this context, the amateur infrastructure of the 1930s could
no longer suffice.

RIGHT: The Dwyryd
Estuary at high tide from
Watch House lawn.

When this you see, remember me
And bear me in your mind
Let all the World say what they will
Speak of me as you find

ABOVE: An early piece of souvenir pottery made by Gray's, designed by Clough for Portmeirion.

Perhaps, therefore, the most far-reaching decision when building work was allowed to recommence in 1953 was to hand over responsibility for retail outlets in the village to Clough and Amabel's daughter, Susan and to her husband Euan Cooper-Willis (the couple had married in 1945). The only existing shop was, Euan recalls, 'hidden away up a dark staircase in Hercules Hall. Few visitors ever found it, and what little takings came in, seemed apt to vanish. This led to the discovery that the hotel barman, a charming Moroccan, had his sleeping quarters up a spiral staircase rising from the shops interior.' Many of the pre-War buildings had had garages built into their ground floors: now these were phased out, replaced by additional accommodation and by properly run shops (starting with the Ship Shop in Salutation), introducing a note of professionalism to the enterprise.

Venturing further afield, in 1958 Susan and Euan opened a Portmeirion shop in Pont Street, London. 'Here can be seen Welsh rugs, tweeds, flannels and tapestry quilts designed by Susan Williams-Ellis,' enthused *The Times*. 'Many of the motifs in carpets and fabrics, and on lustre ware made in Staffordshire, come from her underwater explorations as an aqualung swimmer of note. Coffee tables of Welsh slate are also worthy of note.' For the first time, Portmeirion was being seen in

terms of branding, with a resonance that reached far beyond its own geographical boundaries. Two years later, the couple founded Portmeirion Pottery, a move that was to create an entirely new market for the brand, establishing it on a global basis and becoming for many the primary point of reference for the name.

Meanwhile, the reduction of parking facilities caused by the introduction of the shops had combined with a need to provide proper service access, now that the arches over the main entrance were imposing height restrictions. Susan and Euan suggested a new car park on the far side of the village to be approached by a new road, a proposal at which Clough initially baulked, since it required the removal of some trees, until they pointed out that it would also make a splendid site for a triumphal arch. Suitably inspired, Clough set to work and created something that satisfied his own high standards. 'The Portmeirion car park is, I think, a good advertisement for cautious, selective tree-by-tree clearing, as it really *is* a park – an irregular arena with a central vista ended by a monument, and completely surrounded by fine deciduous trees,' he wrote, adding a characteristically environmentalist note. 'There would seem no good reason why so many parking lots, even in the country, should be the bleak and cheerless deserts that they are.'

ABOVE LEFT: The Triumphal Arch, built in 1962-63 to provide an alternative way in to Portmeirion.

ABOVE: The Salutation Café, pictured here in the 1920s, continued in use as a restaurant until the late 1960s when it became the Peacock Shop.

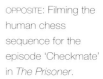
OPPOSITE: Filming the human chess sequence for the episode 'Checkmate' in *The Prisoner*.

'A PLACE OF ISOLATION'

In 1960, the same year that Portmeirion Pottery was launched, ITV broadcast 'View from the Villa', the debut episode of a new series titled *Danger Man*. In it, the central character, John Drake – played by Patrick McGoohan – finds himself in Portmeirion whilst investigating the murder of a banker. It was the first appearance of Portmeirion in a TV drama, and the series itself was the first of the great spy thrillers that were to dominate so much of British television in the 1960s, but more significantly it was the first link between McGoohan and the village: a relationship that was inextricably to link the two in the minds of many.

Danger Man ran for 39 half-hour episodes (including others that were filmed partially in Portmeirion) and then, after a three-year break, returned in a new hour-long format that was sold to CBS in America as *Secret Agent*. This second run established McGoohan as a major international star and, reportedly, made him the highest paid actor on British television. It also provided the launch-pad for the series that was to become his *magnum opus* and the most enduring British cult show of the decade.

The Prisoner (1967–68) centred on a nameless secret agent (or possibly a scientist, it was never fully established) resigning from his job, being kidnapped and waking up in a place known only as The Village, where he is given a new identity: Number Six. In a set-up reminiscent of a cross between Franz Kafka's *The Trial*, George Orwell's *1984* and Mary Wollstonecraft's *Maria, or the Wrongs of Women*, it is never clear where he is, who is imprisoning him or whether the nightmare will ever end. All that exists is the stasis of stalemate: those in authority over The Village want to know why he resigned, which he refuses to reveal, while he seeks to escape his confinement, which they do not allow.

ABOVE: The shelter in which sits the Buddha that came from *The Inn of the Sixth Happiness*, with (above right) Patrick McGoohan as Number 6.

Originally intended as an initial thirteen-part series, it extended out into seventeen hour-long programmes and ended abruptly in 'Fall Out,' an episode that cast more doubt than light over the proceedings. Initial responses were favourable ('a stylish, sophisticated, polished production which goes on where *The Avengers* leaves off,' noted the *Daily Telegraph*), but as the lack of resolution became ever more apparent, it attracted increasing hostility, at least on its first screening. McGoohan recalled the anger of viewers at that last episode: 'Outraged, they jammed the switchboard at ITV: they had been led on, swindled, double-crossed.'

The refusal to explain, the sheer confusion that was engendered, however, have ensured that the series has retained a huge cult following, referenced in other TV shows from *Babylon* 5 to *The Simpsons*, in sitcoms from *Sorry* to *2point4 Children*, in movies from *Brazil* to *The Truman Show*, and – especially – in the work of rock & roll bands from Dr Feelgood to Iron Maiden to Supergrass. Key to its enduring appeal is its external location filming in Portmeirion, a setting both photogenic and imprecise; it was, said McGoohan, who created as well as starred in the series,

RIGHT: The Village with one of the taxis from *The Prisoner*.

ABOVE: *The Prisoner*
campaigns to be
elected the new
Number 2 in the
episode 'Free For All'.

'built in an unusual architectural style, it could well become a place of isolation where people from all over the world could be put away.' Even those who have disliked the place have paid back-handed tribute to its unique atmosphere: 'Clough Williams-Ellis's Portmeirion,' wrote art critic Stephen Bayley, 'an Adriatic Baroque village, built out of scale near Portmadoc, is so terrifying that it was used as the setting for the classic Sixties psycho-drama *The Prisoner*.'

Portmeirion itself wasn't directly identified as the setting until the final episode – 'filmed on location,' read the standard credits – but the publicity for the show made no secret of the connexion, and there is a teasing reference in the episode 'Do Not Forsake Me, Oh My Darling', where an envelope is briefly seen addressed to 'Mr Seltzman, 20 Portmeirion Road'. And while the theme of a man struggling to retain his individuality in a fabricated, faceless world has often been associated with McGoohan's own refusal to play the star system, No. 6's great shout of defiance resonates too with echoes of Clough's own non-conformism: 'I will not be pushed, filed, stamped, indexed, briefed, debriefed, or numbered. My life is my own!'

The Prisoner Appreciation Society – Six of One – continues to hold its annual conventions at Portmeirion, while a shop dedicated to the show has been opened in the village, complete with a plaque commemorating the series. Of more immediate benefit to the resort was the sudden publicity that it gained from being featured on a mainstream TV series: numbers of day visitors doubled in the

OVERLEAF: A rainbow over the estuary, with Watch House in the foreground.

summer of 1968, following the screening. Curiously, the one place where the series couldn't be seen was in the vicinity of Portmeirion itself. It had been commissioned by Lew Grade at ATV and offered to the other regional broadcasters, but TWW, having just lost the franchise for Wales and the West of England, decided against buying the show; it wasn't until 1970 that the new contractor, HTV, screened it in North Wales.

Other filming that has made use of Portmeirion and Plas Brondanw has included Ingrid Bergman's *Inn of the Sixth Happiness* (1958), following which a statue of Buddha was donated to the village, *Dr Who* ('The Masque of Mandragora' in 1976), *Brideshead Revisited* (1981) and the final episode of *Cold Feet* (2002). Frequently used to represent a generic Italian setting, Portmeirion has perhaps been typecast as a location in its own right by its starring role in *The Prisoner*.

BELOW: The fish pond in front of Trinity, one of the original Victorian features, embellished by Clough with a merboy sculpture.

'ANTI-MODERNIST, ROMANTIC AND BACKWARD-LOOKING…'

BELOW: Clough's
preliminary design for
the Piazza, 1925. Brown
ink print with brown pen
and watercolour
(455x685mm). In the
event this design was
never realized, although
the name was revived
in 1965 for the
central space.

The last major change to the structure of Portmeirion
(as seen in *The Prisoner*) was made in the mid-1960s, the
replacement of the tennis-court at the heart of the village by
the central Piazza, a development urged on by Susan and
Euan. Remarkably, Clough was still overseeing all design and
development: he had celebrated his 80th birthday in 1963
with a dinner in the House of Commons, courtesy of John
Strachey, but he remained active both as an architect – his
last work outside Portmeirion was Dalton Hall in Cumbria –
and as a propagandist.

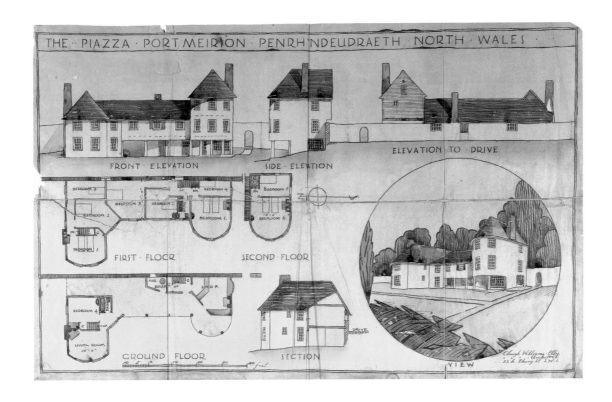

He was still ahead of the game on environmental issues. During his brief tenure at Stevenage he had proposed cycle lanes and the 'pumping of natural heat from the ground for the heating of houses and public buildings,' and in his successful campaign against a proposed massive hydro-electrical scheme in Snowdonia in 1949 he had looked forward to the advent of wind-farms: 'A few years on, or so I am credibly informed, and we shall find our looked for electrical relief coming from wind-driven generators mounted on towers 200 feet high, commonly grouped together in fifties.' In typically scatter-gun form, he had added to these concerns a call for the use of murals in London Underground stations, the teaching of citizenship in schools and warnings about over-population. In 1961 he also became Vice-President of the Advertising Inquiry Council, representing consumers and the public in advertising issues.

By the 1970s, however, even he was beginning to feel the effects of age. 'I used to go around like a circus, or politician, talking to people about the destruction of our surroundings, writing pamphlets and articles,' he commented, regretfully. 'I cannot do so much now, but I am still a general busybody.' Though he himself was slowing down, there were now plenty prepared to pick up the baton. The ecological movement of the 1960s and '70s, and the new economic thinking that drew on E F Schumacher's classic work *Small Is Beautiful*, were perfectly attuned to his thoughts from nearly half a century earlier, and his status as one of the elder statesmen of environmentalism was assured.

In his chosen professional field too, the signs were that the tide was turning in his favour. In 1956 Frank Lloyd Wright, perhaps the only living architect of whom Clough seemed genuinely to be in awe, visited Portmeirion whilst in Wales to collect an honorary degree and, after being shown around, commented to Amabel, 'Why, I do believe you married an *architect*.' But approval from the mainstream of the profession had seldom been forthcoming. Clough's celebration of pleasure, of joy, of life itself was out of kilter with the times for much of his career, as he himself recognized: 'I have great admiration for the modern architects, tackling complex problems,' he commented. 'I only wish I could like what they build. Their work seems to me to be so unfeeling. I have tried to persuade my brethren that men are tender little animals, not machines. Delight has vanished. What makes me angry is that planners and designers are neglecting opportunities to create warmth and human interest.'

His inspiration had always been Georgian, the perfectly proportioned town squares and classic Palladian buildings that had gone out of fashion in the early

ABOVE: Clough in the early-1970s and (above left) with Frank Lloyd-Wright on the latter's visit to Portmeirion in 1956. Bertrand Russell used to say that all you had to do was sit in Portmeirion and in time everyone would pass by.

Victorian period. 'Just before it was all besmirched by the industrial revolution,' he once remarked, 'I do believe that our country stood as one of the loveliest things that God and man had ever made between them.' The modernism of the 1920s seemed, at least for a moment, to offer a return to such civilized values. His 1934 book *Architecture Here and Now*, co-written with John Summerson, even celebrated Le Corbusier's concept of vertical streets, and his own work was not unaffected: the dining room he added to the hotel at Portmeirion very clearly drew on modernism. But the village as a whole made no sense in the context of his contemporaries. 'In the eyes of all right-thinking men,' noted the *Times Literary Supplement*, 'the conception of this ridiculous Welsh fantasy was definitely anti-social and its practical achievement abhorrent.' It added, with a sense of relief: 'Luckily, Clough Williams-Ellis was very far from right-thinking.'

He was, in short, a maverick. As Amabel pointed out, 'He founded no school, didn't seek disciples or colleagues.' And yet his longevity, his consistency, his sheer bloody-mindedness meant that by the 1970s, as modernism began to look vulnerable (a development symbolized by the Ronan Point collapse) and as mavericks began to return to critical approbation, he finally found some recognition. He was belatedly given a knighthood in the 1972 New Year's Honours

RIGHT: The bridge linking
the Round House and
Lady's Lodge looking
towards the Piazza

BELOW: Clough's plan of
Portmeirion in 1929 as
used in the first edition
of the guide book. The
acquisition of Castell
Deudraeth in 1931
gave him access to the
main road and the
Gwyllt gardens were
added in 1941.

List and favourable articles began to appear in the architectural press – some even cited him as an influence on post-modernism. As he commented in 1970, 'I may be anti-modernist, romantic and backward-looking in some of the things I do, but even the moderns of the most severe rectitude come to wallow in Portmeirion.'

Of even more importance, the structures that he had created in the village, and those he had imported, were accorded Grade II Listed Building status in 1971 and, on the advice of his economist son-in-law, Euan, the whole of Portmeirion was placed in a Charitable Trust. Back in 1931 he had been proud to say that 'I have made it an island' – establishing through the use of a Reciprocal Restrictive Covenant with adjoining owners that the peninsular on which Portmeirion stood would not be overdeveloped. Now its future was assured, the buildings preserved against amendment or demolition, and the totality protected from dismemberment.

In 1973 Portmeirion celebrated his 90th birthday with, anticipated *The Times*, 'a two-day event which promises to be the most magnificent birthday party in Wales since one of King Arthur's. And indeed, Portmeirion itself is a modern Camelot.' ('Silly idea,' he remarked. 'They should wait till I'm 100.') Emphasizing that this non-conformist eccentric was firmly part of the national heritage, the statue of a lion that was presented to him was unveiled by Lord Harlech.

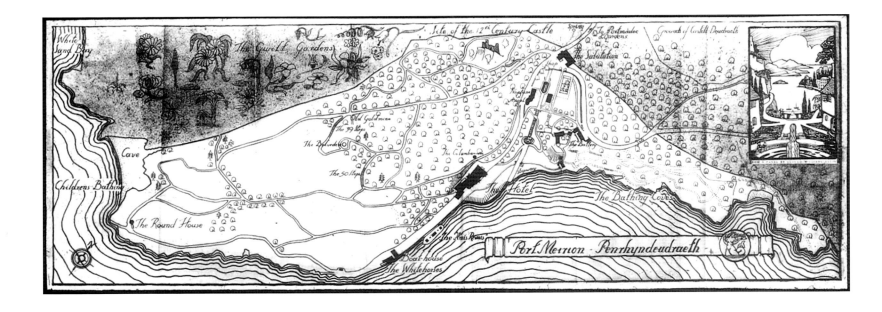

RIGHT: Clough on his
90th birthday, posing
with the statue of a lion
that was presented to
him by his friends and
colleagues to mark
the occasion.

Robert Sakula, who was Clough's personal assistant in the last couple of years, gave some insight into the world that he and Amabel inhabited in the mid-'70s: 'They lived the lives of the landed gentry that, in fact, they were. Even then it felt anachronistic, to the point that I could hardly believe that anyone else, anywhere, could be living the life we led, a sort of 18th-century mythic idyll, simultaneously extraordinary and slightly dull.'

One further building was added to Portmeirion, the right hand tollbooth at the entrance, completed in 1976. In September 1977 Clough made his final broadcast – a Radio 3 talk on the subject of 'Improved Simians' – and in April the following year, at the age of ninety-five, he died.

In *The Pleasures of Architecture* Clough and Amabel had written that 'Puritans, Romantics, and Escapists never are, or even desire to be, at home in the world.' For once, they were wrong. Clough was a pure, unabashed Romantic and yet he was perfectly at home in the world. And, just to be sure, he remade a corner of it in his own image.

RIGHT: View of the
Colonnade, overlooked
by the Chantry.

LEFT: White Sands Bay on the westernmost reaches of the peninsula, with outline of Moel-y-Gest in the distance.

'AN ENCHANTING FOLLY AND THE NICEST HOTEL IN BRITAIN'

In 1984 Robin Llywelyn, the son of Susan and Euan and grandson of Clough, became the managing director of Portmeirion, extending the family connexion into the third generation.

The health of the venture at that stage was mixed. On the positive side, visitor numbers were at an unparalleled height: from 100,000 a year in the early-1970s, they had more than doubled, averaging over 210,000 in the first five years of the new decade. The abrupt rise in numbers during the late-'70s was probably caused by a combination of factors: tourism in North Wales was growing, the death of Clough had brought further public awareness, and a new generation had been introduced to the cult charm of *The Prisoner*, following a repeat screening on ITV (in the days before videos and DVDs, and when there were just three TV channels in Britain, this was a major event).

Elsewhere, however, there was a less encouraging situation. In 1981 a fire had broken out in the hotel – the cause was never discovered – that had destroyed many of the original features, as well as Clough's additions, and had left it unusable. For three years it had stood empty, the blackened walls showing a charred skeleton of a building.

This was, coincidentally, the second great fire to have afflicted Clough's work. In 1951 Plas Brondanw had been reduced to ruins, taking with it virtually all Clough and Amabel's furniture, book collection and drawings. Undaunted, he had rebuilt, despite the austerity restrictions of the period. Now it was time for the hotel to enjoy the same rebirth. The process of re-design and the complications of obtaining planning approvals for a listed building were set in place, and the programme of works began in 1986. Though the impetus was unlooked for, the project did provide an opportunity for rationalization: the original

ABOVE: The two fires –
Clough at Plas
Brondanw in 1951, and
the Hotel at Portmeirion
in 1981.

building had been hurriedly converted from a country house to a hotel, and
additions had been piecemeal over the years; when it finally re-opened in April
1988, it was as a hotel designed and intended for its purpose.

It also re-opened on a new basis. Previously functioning only in the summer
months, it was now reinstated as the centrepiece of the village and was open all-year
round, a fact that reflected the growing diversity of holiday-making within the UK.

Although it had been unprofitable in the years immediately before the fire, the
hotel had always been the anchor that kept the fantastical elements of Portmeirion
rooted in reality, as well as being the precursor of the country house hotels that
would become so fashionable after the Second World War. 'There are those who
think Portmeirion just an *haute-Bohème* piece of garden gnomery,' wrote the *Times
Literary Supplement* in 1963, 'and those who think it an enchanting folly and the
nicest hotel in Britain as well.'

Key to the hotel's success was its cuisine, which Clough admitted took a while to
get right. He never invited the novelist Arnold Bennett to stay, he wrote, because
'I knew he would find fault with the food – and justly; and by the time we had
reached his exacting standard, he was dead.' Bennett died in 1931, giving some
indication of when the kitchen was functioning at its optimum level; by the time
Clough wrote his book on the village, he was able to say with some pride that it had
'a general reputation for really good and interesting food that I think is not undeserved.'

The reputation was indeed impressive. In 1951, just as rationing and austerity
were coming to an end, the writer Raymond Postgate (son-in-law of Labour leader,
George Lansbury, and father of the man who created *The Clangers*) launched the

RIGHT: An early-1960s
photograph over Watch
House (pan-tiled up to
1965, since roofed in
slate) over the old fresh
water, unheated
swimming pool to the
Hotel beyond.

ABOVE: The restored Hotel (post 1988) with the heated swimming pool in the foreground.

Good Food Club whose aims were 'to improve British cooking and service and to communicate to each other information about places where the cooking, cellar and courtesy come up to proper standards.' It was a move that was completely to re-shape public eating in Britain, and Portmeirion featured in the Club's annual publication *The Good Food Guide* from the outset. Mention was made of specialist dishes – 'casserole of duck in wine and cherries, loin of lamb stuffed with walnuts, chicken Valencia, lobster Portmeirion' – and amongst those recommending the hotel was the broadcaster Wynford Vaughan-Thomas. In a later edition there was a further note that 'the beer too is very good'. The status continued in later years ('the setting is beautiful, and service and comfort are beyond reproach,' noted *The Times* in 1968), and care was taken when the hotel re-opened to keep the tradition alive; in 1990 the *Good Hotel Guide* awarded it a César Award, remarking that: 'Phoenix-like, Clough Williams-Ellis's hotel in his exuberant Italianate village overlooking Cardigan Bay has been brought back to life by his grandson after the great fire of 1981. The new hotel is no mere replica of the old, but equally exotic and extravagant in its own way.'

A few other additions have been made to Portmeirion since Clough's time – Susan, for example, designed an extension to the Town Hall and, in 1983, a gazebo to commemorate the centenary of Clough's birth – but the story has essentially been one of modernization rather than new building. Following the

RIGHT: View from the swimming pool lawn up towards Watch House and the Campanile.

hotel re-launch, a massive programme of infrastructure renewal was undertaken in the late-1990s, completely replacing the electrical and sewerage systems: the kind of major works project that is barely noticed by visitors, but essential to the continuing viability of the enterprise.

The need for such improvements had been apparent for some time. For despite his protestations to the contrary ('I am really quite conscientious about dull essentials such as drains,' he claimed), Clough was primarily an architect more concerned with external appearances than the service infrastructure. Indeed, even the internal layout of a building was not always his strong suit; he once, for example, described his agenda for designing a cottage: 'Just one or two general principles. I say: eat where you cook, concentrate on real practical convenience, actual comfort, adequate room, proper equipment.' But in the same context his biographer, Jonah Jones remembers an occupant of one of his buildings being exasperated when sweeping the kitchen: 'Only Clough could have designed a kitchen with eighteen returns to sweep out!'

Further work followed with the complete refurbishment of Deudraeth Castle, which was plagued by dry rot and was also in desperate need of modernization, and then in 2005 with the re-opening of the restaurant, as re-designed by Terence Conran and Benchmark Woodworking.

Other changes too, beyond the physical fabric of the village, were made. In the late-1980s a new company was created, Portmeirion Shops Ltd, which took over the retail outlets in Portmeirion itself and – under the stewardship of Robin's wife, Sian – went on to open a shop in the Wales Millennium Centre in Cardiff, taking the brand name into new fields. Robin himself, a student of Celtic literatures and languages and an acclaimed novelist who first won the prose medal at the National Eisteddfod in 1992, placed a new emphasis by promoting bilingualism in the village, pioneering a development that was to become mainstream.

Through it all, Portmeirion has continued to function in the way that Clough had so wildly dreamed that it could: inspiring a love of architecture and demonstrating that development need not be detrimental to the environment, whilst still functioning as a viable business. It has remained true to the original vision, even though it has subtly adapted itself over the years, its evolution matching that of the nation's holiday habits.

Once it had been the playground of the cultural, if not the financial, elite ('the deserving poor,' as Clough called them: 'approved academics and intelligentsia, especially if with families'). Then, in the post-War era, the visitor-base began to

ABOVE RIGHT: The entrance hall and (above far-right) a bedroom in Castell Deudraeth.

RIGHT: The dining-room in the Hotel, as redesigned in 2005 .

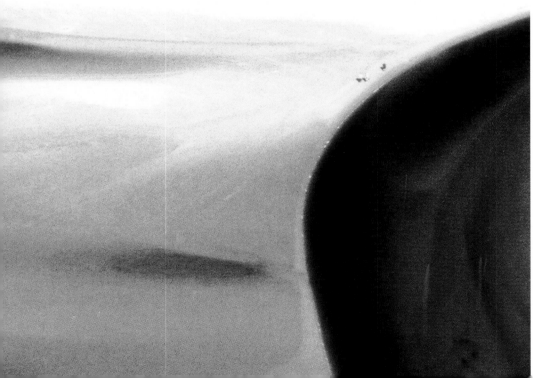

LEFT: An aerial view
of Portmeirion and
its beach at low tide.

broaden, a fact symbolized by the selling off in 1951 of the Mytton & Mermaid Hotel as a halfway house between London and Portmeirion: henceforth it was not simply the metropolitan minority who were to be catered for. In the 1970s the level of self-catering was increased, again reflecting a change in leisure patterns, while the subsequent move to all-year opening allowed for the new pattern of mini-break holidays. It has, in short, been so successful for so long largely because it has had the flexibility to respond to the democratisation of leisure in British society. Similarly, the boost it received from *The Prisoner* was an entirely appropriate reminder of the emerging power of television, and the diversification into pottery and retail was part of the growing awareness of branding.

Meanwhile the village has continued to exert its peculiar fascination in myriad ways. Rock bands from Siouxsie and the Banshees to Supergrass have filmed there, George Harrison chose it as the venue for his 50th birthday celebrations and in 1999 a show garden based upon its fabulous combination of architecture and horticulture won a gold medal at the Chelsea Flower Show.

At the heart of it all, Portmeirion itself remains a defiant statement – eccentric, eclectic and inspirational – of one's man's vision and taste. And it remains an experience so unusual as to be impossible to pin down. It is 'like a giant gnomes' village' said the *Guardian*, whilst the *Sunday Times* declared it 'not so much Italian as madhouse in style, an asylum invented by the maddest inmate'; Lewis Mumford called it 'a museum filled with bits and pieces of the past, put together in the form of a monumental joke, at the expense of the humourless exponents of an abrasive brutalism,' while Bill Bryson referred to it as 'the most magical and ambitious folly built in the last hundred years.' And Amabel was simply amused: 'playing with adult mud pies,' she said.

The last word, however, should of course belong to Clough himself, whose characteristically memorable slogan summed up a philosophy and attitude that continues to enchant and inspire:

Cherish the past;

adorn the present;

construct for the future.

Those individualists, Portmeirion pottery…

POTTERY & GLASS MAGAZINE (MARCH 1964)

PORTMEIRION POTTERY
Mark Eastment

For millions of people around the world, the word 'Portmeirion' evokes images not of the village created by Clough Williams-Ellis, but of Portmeirion Pottery. Some believe the pottery to be made in North Wales, close to or even in Portmeirion itself. What is certainly true is that Portmeirion Pottery will forever be linked to the village, having originated in Clough's desire to create beautiful objects for visitors to the resort, using the creative talents of his daughter Susan and the business acumen of his son-in-law Euan.

Susan Williams-Ellis was born on 6 June, 1918 at Durbins, the family home of critic and painter Roger Fry in Guildford, Surrey. A determined and academically gifted child, she proved from a young age to have an artistic eye combined with a tremendous memory for words and shapes, talents which continued throughout her life. Her love of the Welsh countryside also dated from her childhood, when summer holidays were mostly spent in North Wales, particularly around the family's historic home at Plas Brondanw: it was in nearby Caernarfon that an 11-year-old Susan bought her first antique for 6d, an early nineteenth-century printed mug. She knew early on that she wanted to do 'something in art' and her parents sent her to a succession of schools, before in 1934 they all found exactly what she needed at Dartington School.

ABOVE: Euan Cooper-Willis and Susan Williams-Ellis showing the *Botanic Garden* range in Portmeirion Village, July 1996.

LEFT: Early publicity shot for *Botanic Garden* with Mrs Hey's *Moral of Flowers* book illustrating William Clarke's print of *Rosa canina*.

Dartington was famous for its progressive teaching methods: it didn't have regular lessons and children were encouraged only to go to lessons if they wished to. Among the staff were Bernard Leach and his son David, who taught Susan pottery. One of Susan's earliest carvings, produced in the school's art classes, can still be seen outside Neptune cottage in Portmeirion Village, having been cast in metal by Clough.

In 1936 Susan went to the Chelsea Polytechnic, where she studied under another two impressive and influential teachers, Henry Moore and Graham Sutherland. Art was considered a very suitable subject for girls wishing to study, before going off to get married, and at Chelsea Polytechnic women outnumbered men by five to one. The comparatively few – and keenly sought after – male students included Dirk Bogarde, who studied art before going on to achieve greater fame as an actor.

Susan studied painting (or book illustration, as it was revealingly named) two days a week with Sutherland whose classes were extremely popular. Two further days were spent with Henry Moore, who was responsible for pottery and realism, whilst the remaining day was reserved for life-drawing. As lunches at the Polytechnic were not very good, Susan would join other students with a sandwich and sit by the River Thames or eat in one of cafés in the nearby King's Road who offered spaghetti, then regarded as being rather exotic, to an enthusiastic student market. Her developing interest in all aspects of fine and practical art was noted and a promising career was envisaged, though it was to be interrupted by the start of the war and the resultant closure of the Polytechnic.

During the Second World War, Susan worked for two years for the Air Ministry, an experience that she describes as 'secret, but quite boring'. The most auspicious event of the era came in 1940, when she made a trip to King's College, Cambridge

ABOVE LEFT: Amabel Williams-Ellis in the sea c.1926 with Susan (seated), Christopher and Charlotte.

ABOVE RIGHT: Christopher, Susan and Charlotte Williams-Ellis,1929.

to see her brother, Christopher, and met there his room-mate Euan Cooper-Willis; Susan, according to Euan in later years, was 'initially unimpressed' by him, though after that shaky start a friendship did develop.

After completing a degree in Economics, Euan moved to London to work for the War Office, while Susan did various freelance design work, including an exhibition for the Army Education department that was never used. The couple married in 1945 and moved the following year to Glasgow, where Euan learnt about printing and publishing at the family publishing company, Blackie's. Susan's own freelance career as an artist continued, with her working for a variety of companies and producing, amongst other things, book covers and Christmas cards. Little remains from this period, although one excellent example is the group of twelve tiles commissioned by Elizabeth Denby and produced by Poole Pottery, which was shown as part of a room design in the 1946 exhibition at the Victoria & Albert Museum, 'Britain Can Make It' (to which the wags in that period of Austerity retorted 'Britain Can Make It BUT Britain Can't Have It!).

The couple were keen that their children should grow up in Wales and in 1947 they returned, with daughters Anwyl and Siân, to an old stone mountain cottage on Clough's estate just a few miles from Portmeirion Village. Whilst keeping pigs and growing fruit and vegetables, Euan worked part-time in London as a stockbroker and Susan worked on a range of projects. As well as her book illustration, she designed clothes to help promote Welsh textiles after the War, in conjunction with the Welsh Woollen Industry, and also produced designs for Bernard Wardle's textile and plastic factories in Caernarfon and Manchester. Other design work was done for Dunbar Hay, a fashionable London interior

ABOVE LEFT: Wedding photograph of Susan and Euan Cooper-Willis taken at Plas Brondanw, 29 April 1945.

ABOVE RIGHT: The Cooper-Willis family at Llanfrothen, 1959, (clockwise) Siân, Anwyl, Robin and Menna.

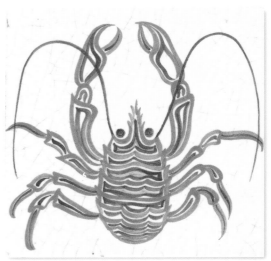

ABOVE LEFT: The façade of the Ship Shop at Portmeirion c.1960.

ABOVE RIGHT: Portmeirion Pottery on display in the Ship Shop c.1965.

RIGHT: 'Sunderland lustre' decorated jug with Susan Williams-Ellis' variation on the Portmeirion mermaid motif.

BOTTOM RIGHT: 'Sunderland lustre' decorated small dish with the *Portmeirion Dolphin* design.

LEFT: Nine of the twelve titles designed for Carter Decorated Tiles (Poole) shown at the 1946 V&A Britain Can Make It exhibition.

decoration and furniture shop owned by Cecilia Dunbar Kilburn and Athole Hay, whilst some of Susan's carpet designs, sold to Wilton and Crossley's, were used in the hotel at Portmeirion.

As wartime building restrictions were lifted and the number of visitors to Portmeirion increased, further accommodation was slowly added to the village and the amenities offered to guests improved. Although Euan was by this time a director of Blackie's and acted as an economic advisor for a London firm of stockbrokers, the greatest proportion of his time was spent working with Clough for Portmeirion. In 1953 Clough gave Euan and Susan control of Portmeirion's general management, their aim being to generate enough money to pay for the continued growth of the village. In particular, Susan took over the running of the one small shop, which was hidden in a corner of the café in Hercules Hall; relocated to a more favourable situation, the Ship Shop, as the new outlet became known, quickly expanded its range of merchandise.

One of the shop's original suppliers was Albert Gray who shared Clough's interest in design. His company, A E Gray & Co Ltd, supplied a wide range of items, including ceramic pieces using old black and white prints, often with Welsh subjects. Other pieces used Susan's graphics, either designed by her or developed by her from one of Clough's original

> I suppose that I am unusual, in that I am one of the few totally independent designers…one of my designs will go through exactly as I see it…then it seems to go like a bomb.
>
> SUSAN WILLIAMS-ELLIS (JUNE 1965)

drawings. These were sometimes combined with a wonderful pink lustre finish known as Sunderland splatter, a style first made popular in the early nineteenth-century. Most of these early pieces carry the Gray's pottery backstamp.

On 1 March 1958, St David's Day, the first Portmeirion shop outside the village itself opened in London at Pont Street, between Belgrave Square and Harrods; it was run by Susan's cousin Sam Beazley who, in his youth, had a promising juvenile acting career, before working for Asprey's. The Portmeirion shop sold modern and antique objects to decorate flats and houses, and the joint venture proved extremely successful and a lucrative outlet for the early Portmeirion ceramics.

With the growing strength of the retail side, and with a continual sense of frustration at being constantly moved to the back of any order-line, an expansion of production was a natural step forward. Gray's Pottery had been founded in 1907 in Stoke on Trent and had employed Susie Cooper between 1922 and 1929, before she left to start up her own pottery. Following Albert Gray's death, Susan and Euan

LEFT: Early-1960s Portmeirion Dolphin apothecary jars.

BELOW: 1960s promotional leaflet for Portmeirion with ranges which used Kirkhams original copper plates or Victorian black and white prints, (left to right) *British Herald, Hunting, Penny Plain Horseman, Penny Plain Pantomime, Comfortable Corsets, Country Life, Sailing Ships* and *Chemist*.

BELOW: Susan's drawing
of a kitchen range
showing the Talisman
design using traditional
Kirkhams shapes
c.1961.

ABOVE LEFT: Apothecary jar in *Moss Agate*.

ABOVE RIGHT: Kitchen cannister in *Malachite*.

bought the company on 1 January 1961 and 'Portmeirion Ware' was born. Exactly a year later, on 1 January 1962, another local firm, Kirkhams Ltd, was bought by them to extend the company's capacity. The combined companies were renamed The Portmeirion Potteries Ltd.

The two firms brought different benefits to the enterprise. Gray's had only ever decorated pieces that were bought-in, whilst Kirkhams was fully equipped to manufacture pottery and had in the past made a fascinating range of pieces: leach and apothecary jars, bleeding basins, chamber pots as well as pestle and mortars. There were, however, teething problems: working conditions at the Kirkhams factory were described by Susan as being 'no less antiquated than pure Dickensian in decay,' and the old bottle kilns, in which all the pieces were fired, had just been declared illegal in the Clean Air Act of 1961, and had quickly to be replaced.

One of the first people to join them in this new venture was Frank Thrower, who became the company's sales and marketing director. A talented designer who had previously worked for Wuidart Glass, a leading firm of Swedish glass importers, Frank continued to buy in Swedish and Danish glass, which was then sold by Portmeirion Potteries to the trade and in their London shop.

Within a very short time, Susan was referred to in the trade press as being 'one of the now-well-known pottery designers', and her work was noted as being 'refreshingly different, reflecting an unusual and welcomed new approach in pottery decoration'. Her early Portmeirion designs such as *Malachite* and *Moss Agate* were innovative but proved challenging to the new company. Both were costly to produce and had a high failure rate, which in turn made them expensive

ABOVE: Frank Thrower advertising Portmeirion Pottery and Dartington Glass whilst in South Africa, November 1969.

RIGHT: Susan's original drawings for *Little Town*, a range which never went to full production but whose shapes were later exploited in other ranges by Portmeirion.

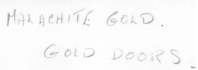

MALACHITE GOLD.
GOLD DOORS.

I mauve   I lime   I grey

ABOVE: *Tigerlily*,
reworking the barge
painting style of
illustration and
Portmeirion's very first
floral design in 1961.

to retail, so neither design, whilst critically acclaimed, was produced in large quantities. Having come into the profession from an art, rather than an industrial design, background meant that Susan learnt her trade as she went along. As designer and owner, she had the luxury of having the final say as to what she produced, with the only restraints being those she imposed on herself. Trying to produce some cheaper ranges using just transfer prints, she created several successful designs, *Waterlily*, *Portmeirion Rose* and *Tigerlily*, which can now be seen as prototypes for some of her later, better-known work.

Susan's design 'eye' and her continued interest in shape development rapidly increased once she had her own production unit to work with. Her priority was to develop her own range of shapes to sell; perhaps having inherited her father's sense of form, coupled with her experience turning wood as a teenager, she soon demonstrated a good feeling for three-dimensional design, an aptitude that was to become her forte.

RIGHT: *Gold Diamond*.
Portmeirion's first multi-
motif pattern with six
different designs on
Grey's undecorated
cups and saucers.

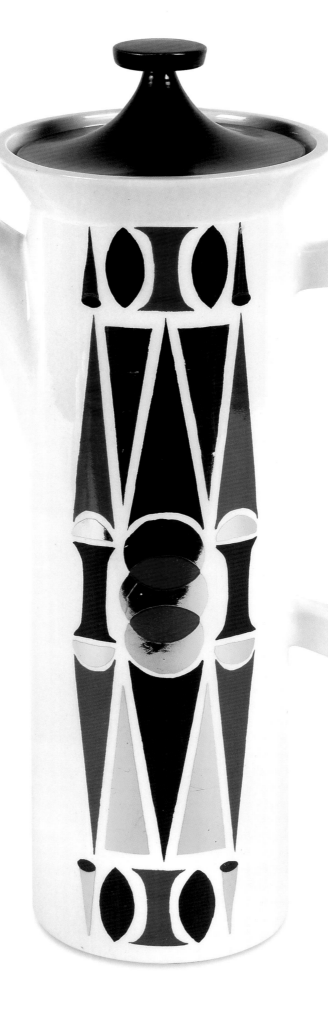

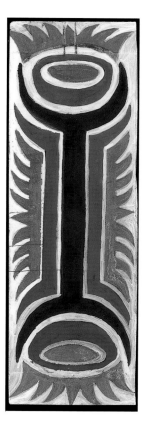
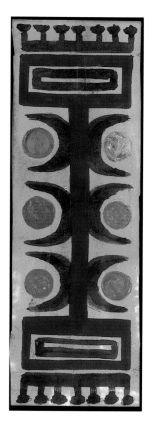

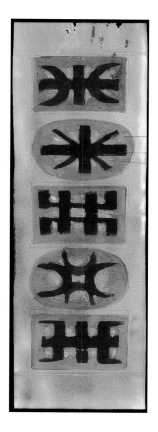

ABOVE: Five of Susan's original designs for the *Gold Six* range, (left to right) *Gold Flame*, *Signal*, *Rule*, *Sign* and *Section*.

One development, which became a classic 1960s design, was an elegant new coffee-pot design which had been made following a request by one of the Portmeirion sales staff. It was created by Susan whilst working with some of the old moulds discovered at Kirkhams, which were cut down into a variety of different sizes. One of these became a 12-inch-tall straight coffee-pot, which could be decorated in a variety of patterns. The first designs, *Gold Diamond* and *Talisman*, sold well but it was *Totem*, introduced in 1963, that brought Portmeirion to the forefront of fashionable design.

To move away from hand-painting, which was expensive, and from screen-printing, which she felt failed to reproduce the delicate brushwork or shades of the original, Susan instead developed a technique she had seen and admired on a Pratt ware teapot bought from a London antique dealer. Pratt ware was a late 18th and early 19th century cream or pearl ware, the patterns moulded in relief and decorated with high temperature underglaze colours. Susan expanded this technique for *Totem*, carving out a design of abstract symbols within a mould. Each piece was then fired after which a single-colour glaze was sprayed onto it. Following a second firing, the result was a lighter tone on the higher parts of the design and a darker one on the lower parts; the fact that the kilns at the time were not even mean that there were also further variations to the lightness or darkness of each piece.

LEFT: A seif shape *Gold Rule* coffee pot from the *Gold Six* range introduced in 1965.

ABOVE: The Pratt ware Teapot c.1795-1815 which was the inspiration behind the raised pattern motif of the *Totem* range.

ABOVE: Three publicity leaflets used to promote the *Black Key*, *Totem* and *Variations* ranges.

Within a few months of *Totem's* introduction, *Pottery and Glass* was noting the success of the venture: 'This company's daring originality and confidence in its own tastes are paying handsome dividends,' and such was indeed the case. Portmeirion Pottery was just starting to make a small profit and Susan's tall coffee-pots were increasing in their popularity with additional new designs, *Tivoli* and *Magic City*. Exploiting additional material from the past, she used Victorian and Edwardian photographs and prints, as well as a variety of typefaces from Victorian ephemera, on an incredible variety of both new and old Portmeirion shapes, all conjured up by her. Some of these pieces can be seen in episodes of *The Prisoner*, and quirky sayings such as DO NOT LIFT BY THE HANDLE or TURN VERY SLOWLY became extremely popular with the youth then enjoying London's 'Swinging 60s' culture. They were also stocked by Terence Conran in his early Habitat stores.

During this time, Susan's own family increased with the birth of a third daughter, Menna, and a son, Robin. Susan and Euan's approach in the workplace was advanced for the time and is still mentioned by workers within the Portmeirion factories. They actively encouraged the use of their Christian names, much to the horror of their French agent who felt that *Madame La Presidente* would have been far more in keeping for Susan. They also actively tried to foster a family atmosphere and were sympathetic to women working around their children's schooling, as well as enabling them to work shifts with their partners. In March 1966 it was noted in the trade press that a Mrs A Williams at Portmeirion Potteries had recently been 'promoted and becomes the first woman graduate work study engineer in the pottery industry'.

RIGHT: Twelve of the many different decorative finishes used by Portmerion on their iconic 1960s coffee pot. Left to right *Corsets*, *Magic City*, *Malachite*, *Royal Palm*, *Gold Sun*, *Where Did You?*, *Montesol*, *Talisman*, *British Herald*, *Queen of Carthage*, *Reddington's Foot Soldiers* and *Tivoli*.

Portmeirion Publicity leaflet c.1975 showing some of the many designs available at this time.

1   Staffordshire Jugs
2   *Botanic Garden*
3   *Botanic Garden*
4   Portmerion Hens
5   Portmeirion Duck
6   *Zodiac*
7   *Oranges and Lemons*
8   *Oranges and Lemons*
9   *Meridian*
10 *Botanic Garden*
11 *Botanic Garden*
12 *Botanic Garden*
13 *Game Pie*
14 *Botanic Garden*
15 *Oranges and Lemons*
16 *Botanic Garden*
17 *Oranges and Lemons*
18 *Botanic Garden*
19 *Oranges and Lemons*
20 *Botanic Garden*
21 *Vine Leaf*
    (a trial range which never
    went into general production)
22 *Strawberry*
23 No name
    (using outside stock
    patterns, primarily for export)
24 *Zodiac*
25 *Botanic Garden*
26 *Gold Key*
27 *Gold Phoenix*
28 *Victorian Embossed*

ABOVE The early 1800 mug with a raised blue sprigged motif which gave the inspiration for the *Meridian* shape.

In 1967 Dartington Glass was established following a meeting with Euan Cooper-Willis and the Dartington Trustees. The glassware was mostly designed by Frank Thrower and distributed by Portmeirion, a mutually beneficial relationship that was to continue for many years.

Susan would often have young designers to work alongside her, one of whom, a rather unique young man, John Cuffley, had a wonderful facility with lettering and line work. His designs included *Zodiac,* a range of twelve Zodiac tankards printed in gold onto matt black and *Gold Phoenix.* His love of music, however, led him to leave the company after just four years to become drummer of the Stafford-based Climax Blues Band (he had earlier played with the pre-Beatles band, Emile Ford & the Checkmates).

Acclaimed in the press, and with an ever-growing order book, times were still comparatively difficult for Portmeirion Pottery. Success encouraged imitators and at one stage there were no less than 50 similar designs to *Totem* being offered to the trade; they may have been of an inferior quality and with a poorer design, but they undermined Portmeirion's position within a competitive market place.

In the early '70s, Susan was asked by her sales team to create a new style of coffee mug and, again, her inspiration came from the past when she found a small Victorian cup, with ridges at the top and bottom and raised design around the centre, at a local antiques shop in Stoke. She worked this shape up into a new range, *Meridian*. Its commercial success was limited because of production

ABOVE LEFT: 1972 A Year to Remember. Susan's leaflet design to accompany the 1972 range of limited edition items produced by Portmeirion. Also the year in which *Botanic Garden* was first introduced.

ABOVE RIGHT: The original *Meridian* range.

RIGHT: Four *Botanic Garden* flowers designs with their first introduction dates into the range. Flowered Chrysanthemum (1994), Virgins Bower (1995), Trailing Bindweed (1972) and Daisy (1972).

difficulties encountered with the glaze, but with some modification (the removal of the ridges), Susan proved she was able to develop new ranges that could be worked around any production difficulties, which would then thrive in the marketplace.

Around the same time, on a visit to the London antiquarian bookseller, Weldon & Wesley, Susan admired, and subsequently bought for 50 guineas, a copy of Thomas Green's *The Universal Herbal* first published in around 1824. The beauty of the prints within the book gave Susan the idea to exploit the past once again, using newly developed printing techniques which enabled the botanical prints to be reproduced on pottery almost in their full original beauty. Portmeirion's new range was born and first shown to the trade in 1972; it was named after an eighteenth-century poem Susan had loved as a child: *The Botanic Garden* by Erasmus Darwin, father of Charles Darwin:

> Botanic Goddess! Bend thy radiant eyes;
> O'er these soft fences assume thy gentle reign,
> Pomona, Ceres, Flora in thy train;
>
> Each circling wheel a wreath of flowers intwines,
> And gemd with flowers the silken harness shines;
> The golden bits with flowery studs are deck'd,
> And knots of flowers the crimson reins connect.

Initially conceived as a coffee/tea set which was to be compact and multifunctional, and using the reworked *Meridian* shape, each piece had a different flower motif on it so that once laid out, they would give an impression of a botanic garden. Initial doubts that the public and retailers would not accept a mixed range were soon dismissed by the large initial orders they received and Portmeirion's *Botanic Garden* range was an immediate success.

Susan continued to use her skills in creating further shapes for the company, turning originals by hand, from which moulds were then produced. Additional books of botanic prints were acquired, so that soon the work of other notable eighteenth-century artists were also added to the range including William Clarke, William Curtis, Louisa Twomley and Albert Jacquemart. The design for the surrounding border on each piece had followed a suggestion by Frank Thrower, who said the designs really needed something to hold the collection together.

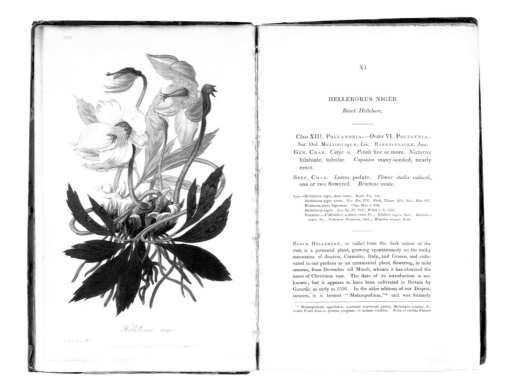

ABOVE: Stevenson and Churchill's *Medical Botany Vol. 1* showing the original plate for the Christmas Rose (*Helleborus niger*) motif first used in the *Botanic Garden* range in 1984.

Susan agreed and made up a simple, but extremely effective green leaf border by repeating a three leaf motif found in a book of leaf forms. She would also take a great deal of trouble with the design of each motif, shaping and adjusting where necessary the plant design to incorporate a bee or butterfly to suit the overall colour and composition.

Up to this time, Euan had supplemented any income from the potteries by working in London four or five days a month and still doing work for Blackie's. Various antiques and artworks, including an early Henry Moore piece, had even had to be sold by them to help keep the company afloat. Now, as the company grew more established, the couple increasingly found that their presence was required more and more at the factory, which worked in split-shifts to keep up with the increasing customer demand. This in turn resulted in the need for major expansion and reconstruction at the potteries in Stoke, including the purchase of new machinery and warehouses as well as a new factory entrance.

Nothing, it seemed, could impede the continued success of the company; even a factory fire in November 1977 didn't stop production for long, with other local potteries helping them out by allowing them to use their kilns. With a bestseller on their hands, Susan and Euan travelled the world, making regular sales visits not only throughout Europe but also to Australia, New Zealand, Canada as well as Hong Kong and the Philippines.

Susan had now been joined in the company by daughters Menna and Anwyl, and together they continued to develop new patterns, *Birds of Britain, Summer*

RIGHT: *Birds of Britain* publicity leaflet from 1978 with engravings from Donovan's 1794 *Natural History of British Birds*.

ABOVE LEFT: The 1982 *Pomona* range using early-1800's illustrations from the *English Pomological Magazine* .

ABOVE RIGHT: *The Compleat Angler* range used Victorian book images as the source material including A F Lydon's Salmon and Trout illustrations.

RIGHT: Kirkhams Leach Jar gave inspiration to the *Botanic Garden* Soup Tureen.

LEFT: *Botanic Garden* in the *Romantic* shape.

Strawberry, Welsh Dresser and *Harvest Blue*. New shapes were also introduced all the time and in 1982 the botanical garden prints were reworked onto a softer and completely new shape known as *Romantic*. Another new botanical range, *Pomona*, was introduced, and around the same time Susan created what she considered one of her very best shapes. On being asked by the American representatives to create a *Botanic Garden* display piece for table and buffet centre displays, she drew inspiration from Kirkhams leech jars, reworked the shape into a soup tureen and added a ladle to go with it. Soon this oversized piece found its way into general production along with other designs from the same period, *Compleat Angler* and *Kingdom of the Sea*, the latter a range only made in very small quantities but developed from Susan's own love of the sea and of the sea life she had been painting for over 30 years.

To increase sales into an already extremely successful US market, a partnership was formed in 1986 between the Naugatuck Triangle Corporation and Portmeirion Potteries Ltd, and soon afterwards, in 1988, the company was successfully floated in order to finance additional expansion, including the purchase of the former Sylvac site in Longton to be used as a casting plant. Recognition of the increasing amount of overseas sales was publicly acknowledged when Portmeirion received the Silver Jubilee Queen's Award for Export in 1990; two years later the company was honoured with a visit by Princess Margaret.

In 1994 Portmeirion China was introduced, using a completely new formula developed by the company that didn't use the traditional animal bone content. Four new designs were used on this, *Ladies Flower Garden* by Susan, *Welsh Wild Flowers* by Menna, and *Ancestral Jewel* and *Summer Garland* by Anwyl. Although by then in her late-70s, Susan still continued to develop various new shapes including *Mandarin* which, using the *Seasons* design of her daughter Anwyl, proved yet again to be a commercial success. This newer, more contemporary collection was further complemented with non-ceramic accessories in glass, metal and even concrete. This shape also led to other new designs, *Dawn* and *Dusk*, being introduced following the same natural design theme.

ABOVE LEFT: Portmeirion Potteries receive the Silver Jubilee Queen's Award for Export in 1990. Left to right, George Hesp, Sir Arthur Bryan, Susan Williams-Ellis and Euan Cooper-Willis.

ABOVE RIGHT: Julian Teed, Product Development Director, and Susan Williams-Ellis show Princess Margaret around the shop whilst on a 1992 visit to the Portmeirion factory.

LEFT: Susan Williams Ellis applying a transfer to one of the vases in the *Botanic Garden* range c.1988.

ABOVE RIGHT: One of Susan's original drawings for the *Mandarin* shape.

BELOW RIGHT: Publicity photograph using the Portmeirion Hotel as a backdrop to the *Season* collection.

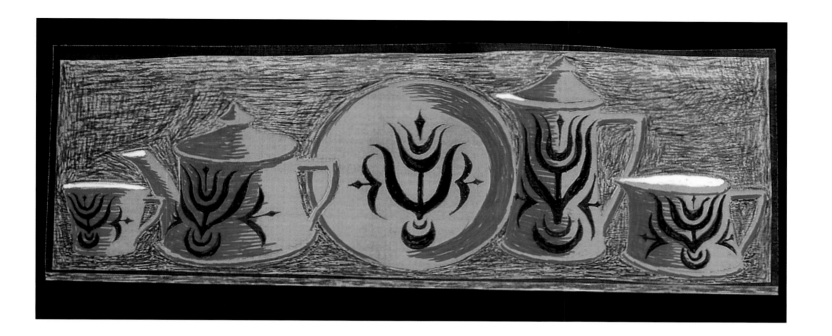

LEFT: One of Susan's original paintings of fish amongst coral in the Indian Ocean.

RIGHT: Susan on one of her many underwater painting trips c.1985.

BELOW RIGHT: One of the limited edition plates produced using Susan's fish paintings.

In its fifth decade, Portmeirion Potteries experienced many changes. Although Susan and Euan no longer had the controlling interest, following the flotation, their influence was felt throughout the company. Susan's major passion for all forms of underwater life, and the incredible collection of paintings made by her whilst travelling the world with Euan, resulted in Portmeirion producing a special limited edition range using some of these images. These were showcased at a special opening in Wales.

ABOVE LEFT: *Up The Garden Path*.

ABOVE RIGHT: *Crazy Daisy*.

Other designers were brought in to work alongside members of the Portmeirion team, all utilising Susan's philosophy that 'good design is good business'. Queensbury Hunt produced a stunning new shape used on *Soho*, following on from Susan's *Mandarin* shape and further opening up their market to a more contemporary customer base. Graphic illustrator, Laura Stoddart launched a quirky giftware range entitled '*Up The Garden Path*' at the beginning of 2006. The company's collaboration with Sophie Conran to develop a completely new range, *Sophie Conran for Portmeirion*, also resulted in a totally fresh look, with each piece designed to have a hand-made feel. The collection brought together the names of two design dynasties, Conran and Portmeirion, and needless to say received great commercial and critical acclaim.

Portmeirion Pottery was at the very forefront of design in the '60s, a market leader following the incredible success of *Botanic Garden* in the '70s, '80s and '90s. Its development of the *Botanic Garden* range resulted in over 60 different plant designs being used since its first introduction in 1972, of which over half were still in production more than thirty years later. With continual change and development of the range each year, new buyers are encouraged into the market whilst discontinued items are readily sold and collected in an expanding collectors' market.

Botanic Garden still accounts for around half of Portmeirion Potteries' total turnover and sales into the UK and US markets remain as strong as ever. In Korea and Japan, a traditional love of all things English, especially in terms of the beauty of nature, have resulted in ever increasing orders. All of this means *Botanic Garden* is set to continue to thrive and develop, and a core part of it will be manufactured at Portmeirion's London Road factory in Stoke for many more years to come.

RIGHT: Part of the *Sophie Conran for Portmeirion* range. Publicity shot 2006.

A glorious jungle of heaths, azalea, mimosa
and rhododendrons. - COUNTRY LIFE, 1930

THE GARDENS OF PORTMEIRION
Stephen Lacey

For work and pleasure, I am lucky to see a lot of gardens around the world, but very few stir me as much as those at Portmeirion. Actually, it was my mother who discovered them for me, while staying as a guest in one of the cottages in the village. The following year, she rented the Belvedere herself for the first week of May, issued the family with a three-line whip, and told us there was a treat in store. That was twelve years ago. We have taken a cottage here every year since.

I am writing this somewhat inebriated. Not on this occasion from drink, but from the potent lily-like scent of a white Maddenii rhododendron, growing in a pot, that I have brought indoors from the greenhouse. It is a plant and a smell that always makes me think of Portmeirion. For if you visit in late April or May, you will meet these rhododendrons in flower, not only dotted through the village among the theatrical follies, but also sprouting from cliffs and mossy ledges in the 70 acres of adjoining woodland, that projects south-westward out to sea.

In my own home patch of North Wales, across the mountains near the English border, Maddenii rhododendrons are not hardy. But Portmeirion, with its generous rainfall and sunshine levels, is lapped by the warm Gulf Stream current, and is little troubled by frost. This allows its planting an exotic edge, which, in combination with its buildings and setting, makes for a very heady experience indeed.

LEFT: Susan Williams-
Ellis' Pagoda above the
Chinese Lake.

ABOVE RIGHT: White
Maddenii rhododendron.

I don't think I have seen any of the many friends I have invited to Portmeirion fail to break into a smile the moment they get down the curve of the entrance drive, and catch their first sight of the architectural ensemble. You have to. Preposterous as it is, this place is packed with *joie de vivre*. And already the planting is contributing to the holiday mood. Colourful Mediterranean shrubs like saucer-flowered cistus and halimium bloom at the base of the cliff beside the drive, in the company of other warm climate plants appreciative of the sunny, well-drained conditions. Early in the year, *Leptospermum scoparium* 'Red Damask' oozes scarlet from dark needle-like foliage, and later the palm-like leaves of *Geranium maderense* will be topped by an eruption of magenta-pink.

ABOVE: Summer bedding of fuchsia with a variegated sycamore behind the Mermaid.

Beyond the gilded Buddha, the planting becomes more esoteric still, with giant violet missiles, up to 12ft high, launched by *Echium pininana* – a Canary Islands relative of our native viper's bugloss – near to the blue and white daisies of New Zealand olearias, and a chunky, sharp-needled, yellow-variegated Mexican agave, protected from too much winter wet by an overhang of rock. Further along, a turquoise-flowered puya may be in bloom, or the double-flowered form of yellow gorse – it gives a double dose of coconut scent.

All this naturalistic planting contrasts with the formal heart of the village, around the Piazza and its bright blue fountain pool. This area, framed by stone walls, incorporates the Victorian walled garden of the former Aber Iâ villa, now the Portmeirion Hotel. The stone lily pond, together with the layout of walls, drives and pathways, is much as it was when Sir Clough Williams-Ellis bought it in 1925, though the site was by then seriously neglected. 'An overgrown jungle,' Clough called it. 'The garden choked with saplings and full-sized forest trees, fallen trunks across the paths, and a great tangle of gloomy laurels denying all view of the sea.'

But in 1861 a local journalist Richard Richards had recorded opening the door into the walled garden and finding a 'very fine' garden with walls 'netted all over with fruit trees'. There was a house, the gardener's bothy, in the centre of the garden (this was 'Cloughed-up' in 1926 and became the Mermaid, a Gothicized

LEFT: Bedding of Impatiens by the Piazza.

OVERLEAF: Two of the
Classical caryatids in
the small piazza by the
Triumphal Arch.

BELOW: Spring bedding
on the Piazza, with
Irish yews and Ionic
columns framing the
Gothic Pavilion.

blue and white cottage), but, wrote Richards, 'Neither man nor woman was there, only a number of foreign water-fowl on a tiny pond, and two monkeys, which by their cries evidently regarded me as an unwelcome intruder.'

Clough put a tennis court into the garden but later replaced it with the fountain pool to open up the core of his Piazza, and the straight pathways were given some Italianate and Riviera panache by having alongside them lines of cabbage palms, *Cordyline australis* – some later replaced by the more reliable Chusan palm, *Trachycarpus fortunei* – and a pleached stilt hedge of beech, underplanted with hydrangeas. This architectural theme was picked up elsewhere around the village and hotel by low, wall-like box hedges, plummeting downhill between daffodil lawns to a shell grotto and look-out platform, by lines of columnar Irish yews, trimmed and corseted to resemble slim Italian cypresses, and by having solitary bay trees sheared into tight cathedral-like domes.

ABOVE: Stone figure of a merboy overlooking the fish pond.

ABOVE RIGHT: Summer bedding of pelargoniums.

Vistas, clipped shapes and architectural objects were Clough's chief interests in a garden. 'He liked flowers, but didn't know much about them,' his daughter Susan told me. He was, however, passionate about trees. 'No good tree is ever molested without good reason,' he wrote in his 'Portmeirion' booklet. 'Trees, therefore, still closely enfold the place.' As he outlines his design principles in his text, you can also glean how integral to his plan he considered the plants and gardens to be. 'A clustering here, a dominant feature there, a connecting link, an axial vista, an interlude of gardens, lawn or woodland, the emphasising of a natural height, the opening of a sea or mountain view, the enclosing of a space.' Every beautiful detail, hard or soft, manmade or natural, was to be harnessed to his purpose.

Happily, Clough's failings as a plantsman have been countered by Portmeirion's gardening staff, who have gradually blended his structural elements with an ever more sophisticated array of flowering plants that exploit the garden's special microclimates to the full. The notable exceptions to this refinement are the central Piazza beds and the slope below Government House, where traditional seaside jollity prevails in the form of bright, swashbuckling bedding plants, with a slosh of garish evergreen azaleas thrown in for good measure! Bring your sunglasses.

RIGHT: Chusan palms (*Trachycarpus fortunei*).

More to my taste is the confection of pastel tints below Telford's Tower and Unicorn where, against a Palladian mansion washed rosy pink, the grass-green, honey-scented Madeiran *Euphorbia mellifera* combines with the soft yellow rhododendron 'Saffron Queen', and explosions of white Maddenii rhododendrons, including 'Harry Tagg' and the potently sweet 'Suave', which opens its trumpets from reddish buds. Elsewhere in the village, look out for 'Logan Early', another rare white Maddenii rhododendron, with huge fragrant flowers in April. Later in summer, the highlights include standard *Hydrangea paniculata* 'Grandiflora', with fat cones of creamy bracts; beside the Mermaid, *Impatiens tinctoria*, a giant 6ft busy lizzie, with scented white, maroon-blotched blooms; and, by the steep drive down to the hotel (where I once nearly lost my front teeth, recklessly testing my nieces' microscooter) an enormous cascade of pink rambler roses, silhouetted against sand and sea.

By 1861, when the lease of Aber Iâ passed from Henry Seymour Westmacott to Captain, later Sir William, Fothergill Cooke, there were also extensive gardens around the present hotel. These sound to be somewhat more elaborate than today's calm sweeps of lawn, gravel and swimming pool. Richard Richards describes a raised terrace, 200 yards long, with 'shrubs, statuettes, and other ornamental appendages', together with a pleasure ground 'which abounds in cascades, water jets, romantic footpaths, and a great variety of costly native and foreign shrubs and flowers.' This connected to 'a number of secluded walks of the most romantic character, leading to elevated spots where the best views may be had.'

Again, by 1925, much of this had become jungle, though legend has it that the network of woodland paths, which survives to this day, was kept open by a lone stag which mysteriously appeared on the peninsula following the death, in 1917, of Aber Iâ's eccentric tenant, Mrs Adelaide Haigh. It was she who turned the gardens into a jungle by refusing to allow the destruction of any plant. When she died, it is said that the hearse could not reach the house until woodsmen had cleared a route through.

But a fine legacy of trees and shrubs from Messrs Westmacott and Fothergill Cooke survived Mrs Haigh's neglect. The village's beeches, tulip tree, variegated sycamore, weeping silver lime and large Scots pine are all Victorian, while around the hotel are old holm oaks and period understorey plantings of evergreen shrubs. It was in this same era that the peninsula, up until then mainly grassy sheep-grazed scrubland with gorse, heather, rock outcrops and patches of native sessile oak, began its transformation into the present wooded wonderland.

Y GWYLLT

BELOW: New Zealand tree ferns (*Dicksonia antarctica*).

While the village conjures up the Riviera, Y Gwyllt (the wild place) plunges you into rainforest. One moment, you are in the Himalayas, in a ravine of rhododendron blossom or ducking under thickets of rhodos so tall you can't see their flowers until they fall to the ground. The next, you are on the Pacific coast of America among soaring, red-barked conifers, or wandering into a gulley of New Zealand tree ferns.

Here and there, there is a temperate interlude, a passage of native beechwood or a view of the sea, and then suddenly a twist of a boardwalk springs the surprise of a Chinese pagoda, and the Welsh oaks give way to eucalyptus and a high plateau of southern hemisphere exotics. In spite of the many times I have walked Y Gwyllt, I still get slightly lost, I still make discoveries, and I am still repeatedly ambushed by its plants and landscapes, which change with every ripple of sunlight and season. I love the luxuriance, the primeval growth, the damp leaf-litter smell, the solitude and the silence broken only by bees, birds and the splash of streams. Indeed, it takes me to as near nirvana as any garden can.

From the village, the most exciting entry point is the pathway between Clough's beech and griselinia hedge, framing stone caryatids and a dolphin fountain, that sits just west of the Triumphal Arch. A new cafeteria has now encroached into this part of the wood, and the magical shock of exchanging bustling Riviera for silent rainforest in a single step has been lessened. But water still gurgles down the slopes, tree ferns and Brazilian *Gunnera manicata*, with huge rhubarb-like foliage, sprout from the shadows, and overhead are the large leaves and massive flowerheads of giant rhododendrons, including *R. falconeri*, with suede-brown undersides to its leaves, reddish-pink *R. griffithianum*, and a superb yellow *R. macabeanum*.

Around Easter time, a twin-trunked tree magnolia, *M. campbellii*, fills the sky with a cloud of pale pink, and over the following months this is succeeded by a mass of creamy flowers on a large, old *Drimys winteri*, and creamy bracts on *Cornus* 'Norman Haddon'. In May the air is injected with the fruity scents of tree peonies and deciduous azaleas, the rhododendron season then continuing with scented white *R. decorum* and *R. auriculatum*. In late summer, there are displays

ABOVE: Gwillt King, a rhododendron hybrid that originated at Portmeirion and won the Royal Horticultural Society's Garden Merit Award in 1938 (the incorrect, Anglicised spelling was characteristic of the period).

ABOVE LEFT: A floral carpet of *Rhododendron arboreum*.

RIGHT: The Gazebo
designed by Susan
Williams-Ellis to mark the
centenary of Clough's
birth in 1983. The central
pillar is one of the old
hotel chimneys salvaged
from the fire of 1981.

TOP: *Magnolia
campbellii* and (above)
*Rhododendron
macabeanum.*

ABOVE: 'Plenty', a sheet metal cut-out by Hans Feibusch with Rhododendron 'May Day' in the right foreground.

from the shrubby horse chestnut, *Aesculus parviflora*, white-cupped eucryphia and, of course, hydrangeas. And in autumn, maple, swamp cypress (*Metasequoia*), and the three tall maidenhair trees (*Ginkgo*) produce striking leaf tints.

All these attractions, and many more besides, are packed into a comparatively small area, making this part of the wood, known as Salutation Wood, rather like an overture introducing the myriad themes to a great symphony. And to jollify the scene further, Clough added a couple of his customary theatrical flourishes in the form of a classical figure (the Silhouette), actually a *trompe l'oeil*, one-dimensional panel of sheet metal – it stands near an old Chusan palm and one of the largest specimens in Britain of *Maytenus boaria*, a suckering Chilean tree of willow-like beauty – and an ornate painted pavilion (the Bus Shelter), made of corrugated iron, where he liked to sit. Each is the focal point of a narrow vista.

Clough did not acquire Salutation Wood until 1940. Indeed before that, his ownership encompassed only the southern/eastern half of Y Gwyllt, up to the line of the dilapidated wall that runs above the present lakes. This lower wood, begun near the village by Henry Westmacott, and then extended westward by Sir William Fothergill Cooke, was much less colourfully exotic – although considerably enriched by conifers (newly introduced into cultivation, and a Victorian passion). By 1925, with the wild oaks seeding everywhere and the laurels and *ponticum* rhododendrons spreading, it had become wonderfully sheltered, but extremely jungly and in parts totally impenetrable.

RIGHT: *Trompe l'oeil* known as the Bus Shelter in Salutation Wood.

LEFT: A bank of
Rhododendron
'Daviesii' with 'Gwillt
King' above.

ABOVE: 'Gwillt King',
Portmeirion's own
hybrid rhododendron
(RHS. 1938).

Susan Williams-Ellis remembers it as a childhood adventure playground – 'Nobody minded children disappearing for hours in those days' – and as a place for picnics, and expeditions to cut down laurels. While her husband, Euan Cooper-Willis, who knew Portmeirion from the 1940s, recalls Clough's enthusiasm for great bonfires – and his failure to notice where the flames were going: 'He once set his coat on fire.'

Meanwhile, the northern/western half of Y Gwyllt had been benefiting from the attentions of Mrs Adelaide Haigh's son, Caton, who, from around 1900, had been indulging in the passion of his era for rhododendrons and other newly introduced flowering species from China and other temperate regions. Many of the plants here are from original wild-collected seed, though sadly there is no accompanying documentation. With the bit between their teeth, Haigh and his gardener Alfred Blount, also bred a superb hybrid rhododendron of their own, 'Gwillt King', still one of the best blood-red varieties available. It may be seen in Salutation Wood and elsewhere in Y Gwyllt.

Haigh's plants, thriving on the shallow, shaly soil, were maturing nicely by the time they came into Clough's possession, though, as everywhere else, even his parts of the wood were now overgrown. Arwel Hughes, still at Portmeirion and now Head Gardener, remembers Clough – 'arriving every afternoon around 2pm in his soft-top Triumph Herald' – enthusiastically watching the clearance of pathways through Salutation Wood, over which his architectural eye-catchers would shortly dominate.

Penetrating further into Y Gwyllt, Salutation Wood's lush opening salvo of broadleaved evergreens, grassy glades and water is exchanged for a dark, needle-strewn grove of enormous conifers. *Cryptomeria japonica* 'Elegans', with feathery foliage, and western red cedar, *Thuja plicata*, have both made wide-spreading, fat-limbed trees, and as you explore, you move on to meet impressive specimens of redwood, wellingtonia, firs, pines and Lawson cypress.

The reward for taking the path up to Castle Rock is the best bird's eye view of the village and estuary. This bluff is presumed to be the site of the twelfth-century Castell Deudraeth, built by Clough's ancestor, Gruffydd ap Cynan, King of North Wales, but all traces of it were removed by Sir William Fothergill Cooke 'lest the ruins should become known and attract visitors to the place'. Instead, the dominant building is now the gazebo, erected in 1983 to celebrate the centenary of Clough's birth.

BELOW: *Cryptomeria japonica* 'Elegans'.

ABOVE: *Eucryphia cordifolia*.

RIGHT: A classical temple sited by Susan Williams-Ellis above the lesser of the two lakes with giant leaves of *Gunnera manicata* below.

Low-growing evergreen azaleas, dwarf rhododendrons and heathers cloak the Rock, in the company of eucryphias, a splendid palm-like daphniphyllum, and a large, multi-stemmed *Magnolia acuminata*, known as the cucumber tree on account of its long, slender fruits, which was planted here in Victorian times. And from the summit, there is a fine view down over the first of Y Gwyllt's two lakes, Temple Pond, marked out by Clough and landscaped under the supervision of his daughter Susan in the 1960s.

A particularly atmospheric little pocket of rainforest is to be found nearby, signalled by an opening in the undergrowth which leads over mossy, leaf-littery ground into a tiny dell, across a stream, and onto a winding boardwalk. En route, you pass small yellow-flowered rhododendrons, *R. sulfureum* and *R. valentinianum*, growing on tree stumps as they would in the wild, finally emerging from the shadows beneath a superb, giant-leaved *R. falconeri*. In fact, as in many other parts of Y Gwyllt, the rhododendron lover now finds himself in rhodo heaven. All about this area, there are excitements: a bank of purplish-flowered *R. dauricum*; lemon 'Parisienne', 'Saffron Queen', and white Maddenii varieties growing on rock faces; and chunky plants of winter-flowering 'Nobleanum' (an enormous old survivor), white *R. decorum*, pink *R. montroseanum*, and elephantine-leaved *R. sinogrande*.

Here and there, you catch sight of the true giants, 'Cornish Red' (Smithii Group) varieties of tree-like

ABOVE: Hydrangea 'Générale Vicomtesse de Vibraye'.

proportions, flaunting deep pink, football-sized flower trusses in spring. Above Temple Pond, you stroll into a tunnel of them, their trunks creating a patterned palisade beneath the canopy of leaves. Pale pink and rich red forms of arboreal rhododendron also rear up between the trees, and there is a fine group of 'Argosy', a large hybrid with white, scented trusses in late summer. It is ambush after ambush.

I have not yet mentioned camellias, which are also hereabouts in thickets to enliven the winter and spring season. These include numerous old varieties of *C. japonica*, singles and doubles in white, red and pink. As you approach Temple Pond, herbaceous plants again start to contribute to the leafy luxuriance. Yellow- and white-flared skunk cabbages (*Lysichiton*) colonise the pond's margin, and a great raft of the largest of all waterlilies, *Nymphaea* 'Gladstoneana', floats on the open water. While from the upper path, you look down on the massive umbrella foliage of *Gunnera manicata*, and the traceries of giant fern fronds, including ground-arching *Blechnum chilense* and the tree fern *Dicksonia antarctica*.

There are more big ferns along the path through Cliff Wood, where oaks stretch mossy limbs beneath a wall of grey rock, accompanied by some fine conifers, *Thujopsis dolabrata*. This is a dreamy stretch of planting, with scattered drifts of skimmias, seemingly never without red berries, enlivening an otherwise fairly monochrome scene of greens, whites and summer blues – these last supplied by lacecap and mophead hydrangeas, such as 'Blue Wave' and 'Générale Vicomtesse de Vibraye', which are principal suppliers of late colour through Y Gwyllt. A huge plant of the rambler rose 'Brenda Colvin' also contributes a snowdrift of summer white.

Dicksonia antarctica is here joined by other tree ferns, while nearer ground level the most enormous fronds come from the hardiest of the chain ferns *Woodwardia unigemmata*. Accompanying them are many smaller ferns, including the native polypody which colonises the branches of the oak trees. For the eagle-eyed observer, there is a big surprise, for also growing epiphytically among the polypodies are some much more unusual plants, *Fascicularia bicolor* and *F. pitcairniifolia*. These hardy bromeliads have their star turn in the autumn, when the bases of their slim, prickly leaves turn dazzling scarlet.

It takes a real plantsman to think up, and then to execute, such a piece of planting. For this, and most of the other magically naturalistic plantings in Y Gwyllt and the village over the past quarter century, we can thank one of

Portmeirion's gardeners, the botanist Philip Brown. His encyclopaedic knowledge, especially of rhododendrons, combined with his sensitivity to landscape (letting each site dictate its own theme and mood, and never over-egging the cake with suburban colour mixtures), attention to detail, and intimate knowledge of every nuance of habitat available at Portmeirion, not only enabled him to introduce and triumph with rare and tender species, but also to make it look as if every plant belongs here, is happy, and has arrived by itself. It is this which, for me, distinguishes these gardens and elevates them above other great woodland and seaside gardens I have seen around the world.

BELOW: Tree ferns *Cyathea dealbata*.

Philip retired in 2002, and I miss the two-hour guided tours he gave me, and the vase of rhododendrons, accompanied by copious handwritten notes, he always put in our rented cottage just prior to our arrival. For his successors, his is a hard act to follow, but I am putting my trust in them to learn from him, and keep Portmeirion on its pedestal.

A cluster of Philip's scented Maddenii rhododendrons, including a good compact form of blush-pink *R. edgeworthii*, are perched on an outcrop at the western end of Cliff Wood, and from here you have the choice of either continuing on downhill, veering southwards down a shady track, or climbing to the north up a steep, stone stairway. Going downhill, you pass a hollow below the rock face – a sheltered spot exploited to grow heat-seekers like ferny-leaved acacias and grevilleas, and paddle-leaved *Magnolia macrophylla*.

The path then plunges to the Ghost Garden, so named by Clough not because it was haunted, but more prosaically because it was the remnant, or ghost, of the garden belonging to the Old Ferry Cottage (Trwyn y Penrhyn), which was abandoned following the building of the Cob across to Porthmadog. Nevertheless, the ghostly theme has been taken up in the planting of a collection of pale-trunked, silvery eucalyptus species to join the Victorian monkey puzzles, Monterey pines, self-seeding berberis and daffodils.

There is, however, a pocket of wood that on occasion may well ring to ghostly howls. That is the Dogs' Cemetery, a legacy of Mrs Adelaide Haigh, who preferred dogs to people. The shady track leading to it is lined with Chilean lantern trees,

ABOVE: Headstone in the Dogs' Cemetery.

ABOVE LEFT: 'Gwillt King' with the estuary beyond.

LEFT: A beech avenue in the Gwyllt.

Crinodendron hookerianum, dark evergreen shrubs which drip in early summer with bauble-like flowers in an appropriate blood red. The adjacent areas were overgrown and clogged with cherry laurel and *Rhododendron ponticum* until cleared in the 1980s when, following Clough's death, Susan Williams-Ellis instigated a programme of regeneration under the then head gardener Geoffrey King. Many fine old specimens were discovered still alive in the jungle, including in this area, among the pines and larches, these included scented white *R. griffithianum* and *R. maddenii* ssp *crassum*, and a huge red-bracted *Pieris floribunda*.

Taking the stairway, you pop out above the cleft in the rock into another planting of distinctive character, framed by sessile oaks. This is Exotic Hollow. In early summer, the first ambush is from the Chilean flame tree (Embothrium), bristling in scarlet, and around the corner, this southern hemisphere theme is pursued with the likes of ferny-leaved *Gevuina avellena* and *Lomatia ferruginea*, southern beech (Nothofagus), white-flowered eucryphias, and monkey puzzle. What really strikes the different note is the preponderance of grassy and sword-shaped vegetation at ground level, everything from broad-leaved phormiums and silver astelias to white-flowered libertia, pink-belled diarama, pampas and tussock grasses, with cordylines rising above. These also fringe a small pool. The planting was modelled by Philip on photographs of sub-montane forests in New Zealand.

From here, you can double-back east, down an azalea walk (like camellias, evergreen azaleas were planted in great drifts by Caton Haigh) and on into rhododendron woods, or you can continue along the boundary wall (the gorse and rock-strewn pasture on the other side giving you a taste of what Y Gwyllt would also once have looked like) to the north-west corner of the property. The long path, undulating uphill and down, first past new plantings of rhododendrons and azaleas and then becoming wilder, keeps its secret, until suddenly you emerge from the shadows onto open headland. In front is the breathtaking panorama of Tremadog Bay. After all this time spent walking under the canopy, walled in by trees and cliffs, the thrill of such a broad view is intensified.

BELOW: View from the end of the headland towards Borth-y-Gest and Porthmadog.

ABOVE: One of several
Victorian hides used for
pheasant shoots, this
one is near the Dogs'
Cemetery.

Another viewpoint presents itself as you continue on the circuit, a spot known as the Pagoda, but actually just remnants of a stone building, presiding over a drop onto an inaccessible wooded flank of peninsula and a sweep of sand and sea. But there is another highlight to this area: a tunnel of *Rhododendron* 'Cornish Red'. This is the most bewitching of the several avenues of it planted by Caton Haigh, having become a fairytale tangle of twisted trunks and mysterious depths, humming with bees and carpeting the paths with pink trumpets in early summer. Children love it, as Robin Llywelyn, Clough's grandson, remembers from his own childhood, when 'Y Gwyllt was full of dark, exciting tunnels, and so few visitors ventured in there, it was so easy to get lost.'

From the narrow stairway now taking you downhill, I usually make a small digression to the stone shelter under the cliff (very handy in a shower), opposite which there is an open maquis-like bank of heathers and aromatic cistus, above scattered acacias and eucalyptus. And then it is back to the stairway, where one of Y Gwyllt's most famous apparitions looms. Named the Dancing Tree by Clough for its constant movement in the breeze, it is in fact a New Zealand griselinia of gigantic size, the oval grass-green foliage complementing stout dark trunks and the ground round about (and indeed its own limbs) sprouting forests of its own seedlings. It is thought to have been transplanted here by Sir William Fothergill Cooke when he built the steps.

Hemmed in by woods and rock, you are enticed to venture down a couple of spurs off the main pathway, and another great *coup de theatre* is sprung. Suddenly, you are in a valley bowl, looking over a panoply of flowering shrubs. Inspired by a trip to Yunnan in China, Philip Brown seized on the opportunity to create an entire naturalistic landscape of rhododendrons largely from scratch. On the upper ridges, dwarf varieties, appreciative of the exposure to the sun and accompanied by scented white Maddenii varieties, are grouped into confections of purplish blues, pinks and other tints. And these flow into pockets of taller rhododendrons, such as violet *R. augustinii*, pale yellow *R. lutescens*, and lavender *R. oreotrephes*, with glaucous foliage. It is a wash of pastels, with 'Moonstone' and 'Cowslip', oval-leaved *R. williamsianum* hybrids, picking up the theme in the gulley below.

BELOW: *Gunnera manicata* in Shelter Valley.

OVERLEAF: View over the
Chinese Lake.

RIGHT: The bridge over
the Chinese Lake.

This, Shelter Valley, takes its name from the stone shelter that stands at the base of the opposite hillside. Looking down on it, you see the bold foliage of tree fern and gunnera luxuriating behind a wall nearby. While the views of the slopes above, clad in *Rhododendron* 'Sulphur Queen' among other delights, is framed by pines and tall eucalyptus, *E. coccifera* and *E. glaucescens.*

A stream plays down the valley, and following it uphill you come to the larger of the two lakes. Also dug in the 1960s, and re-excavated and lined in the 1980s, it is now a broad, glassy expanse of still water and reflections. The principal eye-catcher is the red Chinese Ting pavilion, designed by Susan Williams-Ellis, perched on the rock outcrop which divides the lake into two parts. A matching Chinese bridge links this to the lake's southern shore, while the pathway

BELOW: A water lily
(*Nymphaea*
'Gladstoneana') on the
Chinese Lake.

BELOW: White Sands Bay on the south western tip of the peninsula.

around the outcrop snakes between Japanese azaleas and Japanese maples which, with the neighbouring birches and other trees, give a bonfire of autumn tints. Leaning on the sides of the bridge, you can idle the time watching the fish, and the dragonflies alighting on the marginal plants, which include iris, astilbes, candelabra primulas, white skunk cabbage, and pink persicaria. Native waterlilies and nuphars float on the lake's surface, and daffodils abound in spring.

There is contrastingly rugged drama on the north shore, where several massive, large-leaved rhododendrons, purple-flowered *R. protistum* and cream-flowered *R. sinogrande*, punch dark shapes into a great chunk of exposed cliff face. Other big varieties in this area include rose-red 'Russellianum', yellow *R. macabeanum*

and clusters of seedlings – for big-leaved rhododendrons seed freely at Portmeirion. Camellias are also here in variety, together with an exceptionally elegant and dashing *Rhododendron cinnabarinum* hybrid called 'Cinnkeys', which so far has not fallen prey to the deadly mildew disease to which this tribe of rhododendrons is sadly prevalent. Against a blue sky, its bunches of orange, yellow-tipped bells are an absolutely stunning sight.

The ridge on the southern side of the lake, Battery Ridge, offers a network of steep narrow tracks demanding exploration. Many more camellias are here, among the heathers, vacciniums and other shrubs, and if you continue on towards the village, you will come to a lovely patch of beechwood, its bright young foliage well partnered in early summer with violet *Rhododendron augustinii*. The far section of the lake is now crowned with a new pavilion by Susan Williams-Ellis, called Flora's Seat.

But to complete the circuit of Y Gwyllt, you need to turn back, ascend the south side of Shelter Valley, curve down beside the new plantings of skimmias and hydrangeas, and find the pathway to the lighthouse and the beach. This is another magical walk, down a narrow sandy track between scented gorse and estuary, full of birdsong. The wood has been left quite natural to merge with the landscape beyond, though here and there, a sympathetic exotic such as cistus or olearia was stirred in for spice, and to pick up the tints of the wild thrift growing on the shoreline rocks.

OVERLEAF: The framed
view over the sunken
lawn towards the
summit of Cnicht.

PLAS BRONDANW

The gardens of Plas Brondanw seem to be an even better
kept secret than those of Y Gwyllt. Almost every time I have
come here, there hasn't been another visitor in sight. And
yet, they are hardly more than a couple of miles away, off
the road to Beddgelert. You know when you are getting
close, because Clough's trademark turquoise-blue paint
starts appearing on the windows of the roadside cottages.
Then comes a handsome stone gatehouse, and you turn the
corner to be greeted by a stylish little flourish of pleached
limes and topiaries.

The hand of the Master, blending Italy, Wales, whimsy
and wit, is immediately identifiable, but there are striking
contrasts to Portmeirion. The dominant natural presence is
no longer the sea, though before the building of
Porthmadog's Cob that did once sweep up the valley and lap
the base of Plas Brondanw's west-facing slopes (Clough
decided to commemorate this with mermaid and dolphin

LEFT: Topiary at Plas
Brondanw.

BELOW: The steps up to
Clough and Amabel's
private lawn directly in
front of the house.

ABOVE AND RIGHT: Plas
Brondanw was, wrote
Clough, 'a passion, an
obsession if you like.'

details in the garden gates). No, here the great presence is the mountains, which loom large in the middle distance. Clough thought, probably correctly, that early visitors to the house, built by his ancestors around 1550, would have considered this an eccentric choice of site, for in those days mountains were not objects of beauty, but viewed as threatening and savage.

But for Clough, who inherited the property from his father 'as a sort of twenty-first birthday present', the drama of the landscape was to be relished. Like many of his era, he was under the spell of Italy, and for an Italianate garden of formal terraces, and dark, narrow corridors opening onto epic panoramas, what better spot could be imagined?

But, he wrote in *House and Garden* magazine in 1976, as a young architect, just starting up in practice and with no appreciable income, 'the recreation of the garden setting had, perforce, to be very much a step-by-step affair. That, of course, gave much time for thinking, though I decided the outline of what I ultimately aimed at almost at once, and drew up a scale plan to which I have adhered throughout, as I proceeded gradually to fill in the picture. A ten-pound cheque, and I would order as many little box or yew plants as that would pay for; one for twenty, and that much worth of long-awaited paving or steps would materialize.' More than at Portmeirion, the gardens were his own personal project, and he worked on them between 1908 and 1914, and periodically thereafter, for this was his home all his long life.

ABOVE LEFT: Steps and
flaming urns marking
the grave of Clough's
dog Pennant, killed in
the fire of 1951.

ABOVE RIGHT : A
renaissance figure atop
an Ionic column at Plas.
The other columns are
at Portmeirion.

The metal entrance gates – turquoise-blue, of course – are solid, too tall to see over and usually closed, and with anticipation charged, it is a bit of a disappointment to pass through and find yourself in the service yard ! Never mind. A few more steps on, and you are smiling in front of a splashing fountain of a boy, wearing a outsized fireman's helmet and attempting to extinguish the flame-coloured goldfish with a length of fireman's hose. The inscription around the base reads 'Clough Williams-Ellis inventsit/Trustee Potters Arts Guild sculptsit'. I failed my O-level with this sort of Latin.

As at Portmeirion, Clough sets a light-hearted tone, and this ripples around the two-acre site, especially in the wonderful topiary yew and cypress parliament of pinnacles, rockets and cake-stands. These congregate in the southern half of the garden, combining with stone urns raised theatrically high, and the pleached limes which, now old, mossy and with little need of support, add their own curious, knobbly silhouettes – echoed in the mophead hydrangeas, which were a Clough favourite. All this creates what has to be one of the wackiest skylines in any British garden, and softens the sharper elements of Italianate design with a good dose of eccentric, homely charm.

LEFT: The steps up to
Clough and Amabel's
private lawn directly in
front of the house.

ABOVE: A wrought iron
crown above a pair of
gates designed by
Clough.

RIGHT: The view to the
North through a frame
of pleached limes
towards the summit
of Cnicht.

A grass corridor, falling and rising again via stone steps
and balustrades (turquoise, with mustard-gold finials – the
Plas Brondanw livery), leads under a lime arch to a viewing
platform, the Apollo Belvedere, over the valley marshes.
There are rhododendrons and scented azaleas interspersed
with the topiaries along the corridor, with climbing flame
flower *Tropaeolum speciosum* putting scarlet gashes through
the yew. And at the head of a cross-axis stands a stone arch
adorned with classical busts – mirrored opposite by arched
hedge-openings framing views of the mountain Moel Hebog.
I like the contrastingly intimate scale of this whole area.

Off the corridors you are enticed into little rooms, the
principal one being filled by a shallow pond with a central
column bearing a miniature-sized Roman centurion. The play
of levels, terraces, steps, pools, paint colours and ornament,
is continual, busy and entertaining. This is calmed down
somewhat by repetitions of plants – hostas, roses, camellias
and hydrangeas featuring strongly. That works well. Menna
Angharad, Clough's granddaughter, has been refreshing the
planting at Plas Brondanw since the mid-1980s.

LEFT: Cnicht, sometimes known as 'the little Matterhorn', framed by Clough's topiary. Clough owned the southern slopes of the mountain, seen here, which he bought to protect it from exploitation.

RIGHT: With the correct water pressure the fireman fountain created the illusion of a liquid volcano emerging from the summit of Cnicht if viewed from the southern end of Plas garden.

BELOW: A wrought iron gate designed by Clough and made at the foundry in Porthmadog, leading into the woods next to the chasm at Plas Brondanw.

A large stone Orangery signals a change of scale, and you descend onto an enormous rectangle of lawn, sandwiched between the house above and a hedge running below. This hedge terminates in a column raising aloft the Emperor Augustus – backed by an enormous, triple-trunked horse chestnut – and a delightful turquoise and gold clairvoyee gate, which holds the distant mountain Cnicht, known as the Welsh Matterhorn for its pointed summit, in its curved embrace. In the centre of the lawn, a vast evergreen oak grows from a stone balustraded podium, and in spring the spongy grass around the old apple trees – the rainfall is considerably higher than at Portmeirion – is studded with wild Lent lilies, *Narcissus pseudonarcissus.*

Directly in front of the house is a truly commanding gesture, a 100-yard runway of slate slabs, extending from the service yard at one end, under the arch of the house's buttress wall, to the garden's boundary corner. It is considered one of the greatest vistas in British gardens. A cross axis cuts into the hillside just behind the house, on the other side of the road, formalising and absorbing the outside landscape into the design. Though not obvious to the visitor (because the house courtyard is not open to the public), there is a similar, but even more impressive vista from the front door. This takes the form of a rising avenue of shaped trees carved into the woods to the south. You can walk up this via a gate by the road, and the rewards are a cascade plunging into a dark chasm, and a flaming urn monument commemorating Brondanw's triumphant revival after a disastrous 1951 fire. Further on is an outlook tower, with views to the sea.

Back inside the garden, you process along the slate corridor and yew hedge past a succession of entertainments: thin rivers of astilbes, white Japanese anemones and shuttlecock ferns, a cluster of weeping cherries, a bean tree (Catalpa) and a bust of Inigo Jones. Finally, you arrive at a circle of lawn, scented with azaleas in early summer. From a low stone wall, water trickles from a lion mask into an arched pool. Alas, the miniature statue of Peter the Great, which once crowned this wall was, like Apollo at the other end of the garden, stolen a while ago (an all-too common hazard nowadays). But you will be happily distracted, for behind rise the triple Moelwyn peaks, with, on a clear day, the summit of Mount Snowdon itself in the distance, regularly snow-capped.

Clough called Plas Brondanw 'an architect's garden', and indeed, in many ways it is the perfect counterpart to Portmeirion, its walls, towers and pinnacles built of yew, its spaces quieter and more ordered, and its design and content more deferential to its majestic setting. They are some duo!

LEFT: This flaming urn above the chasm commemorates the restoration of Plas Brondanw following the fire of 1951 and lists the names of all the men involved in the work.

If you require a monument, go to Merioneth and look at him. - THE TIMES, 1971

THE BUILDINGS OF PORTMEIRION

Robin Llywelyn

Portmeirion is normally described as Italianate, but while that gives some indication of the overall feel, it is insufficient to capture the full range of architecture. As Clough's friend, the sculptor Jonah Jones, wrote: 'It is a delightful hotchpotch of sometimes disparate structures, Bavarian vernacular, Cornish weather-board, Jacobean, Regency, Strawberry Hill Gothic and even Victorian Gothic.'

The mixture of styles is an integral part of the charm of the place, giving it a breathtaking diversity and scope as Clough cast his eye over the centuries of architectural design. 'In the early days,' noted *Country Life* in 1976, 'Portmeirion was often compared to an Italian village, but as the years pass it will look more and more "Cloughish" and expressive of its two generations.'

The village was built in two stages: from 1925–39 the site was 'pegged-out' and its most distinctive buildings erected; from 1954–76 he filled in the details. This second phase features some classical and Palladian constructions which contrast with the Arts and Crafts style of earlier buildings. In addition, several of the structures were salvaged from demolition, hence Clough's description of the place as 'a home for fallen buildings.'

Portmeirion gave Clough pleasure and he hoped that it would give pleasure to others. It encapsulated his lifelong pursuit of beauty, 'that strange necessity.'

LEFT: Detail of Clough's 1935 drawing for the Observatory Tower.

ABOVE RIGHT: Wind vane on the top of the Bell Tower.

TOLLGATE

Portmeirion's twin Palladian tollbooths were built more than twenty years apart. The right hand one was Clough's very last building, completed in 1976. Its companion was not built until 1999.

The location of Portmeirion's tollgate has changed over the years. In the early days the toll barrier was at Toll House in Battery Square where day-visitors were invited to ring a bell for the gatekeeper. Numbers grew during the 1950s and new car parking and catering facilities had to be developed, along with a new tollgate, built in the style of a truncated tower. A 1930s sheet metal mermaid once used on the Observatory Tower now occupies an archway here, up a flight of cobbled steps.

SECONDS WAREHOUSE

Next to the tollgate is the Seconds Warehouse which sells Portmeirion Pottery. This was previously the estate garage. Behind is Smith Square, where offices and workshops are housed around the estate yard. This was built by Clough's master joiner Mr Braund-Smith and completed in 1971.

Built for functionality these service buildings exemplify Clough at his most basic and yet they do not lack for a certain elegant symmetry. The murals to front and rear are by Nigel Simmons.

CHANTRY LODGE

Chantry Lodge (1969, listed Grade II, 1971), pictured above, as the Reception is properly known, was designed in 1968 as a simple two storey house of domestic character. Front casements to the first floor have diamond panes typical of Clough's work. The arched doorway is left of centre with another arch opening on the first floor and an arch opening onto the estate yard. Chantry Lodge is used as the main reservations and reception office for the village.

CLIFF HOUSE

Opposite Chantry Lodge is Cliff House (1969) which was Clough's last large fully detailed building at Portmeirion, designed in August 1967, with the Cliff House Annex subsequently designed in November 1970. Like many of his buildings during this period Cliff House is a neo-classical Georgian style house with several features typical of Clough's work such as the trompe l'oeil windows covering the entire north facing elevation and half of the west elevation. This was to provide privacy for the occupants of the cottage while at the same time adding interest to an otherwise featureless facade.

The statue outside Cliff House is the Huntsman, presumed English, c.1750, though it is so severely eroded that identification would be impossible; evidently the Huntsman had been standing in an unsheltered position prior to his relocation to the Cliff House in 1969.

GROTTO

Immediately below Cliff House, reached via steps from the Gate House and through a slate archway, is the cliff top Rotunda or Grotto (1954, listed Grade II 1971). It comprises a lookout platform above a shell Grotto.

This semi-circular single storey flat topped structure with central armillary sphere was built to add an intriguing item to the Portmeirion panorama from the sea, and also provides a commanding viewing platform overlooking the whole estuary. Seen from the sea it resembles a defensive bunker or lookout post guarding the shoreline. The shell grotto contrived beneath it has five openings and its walls and ceiling are inlaid with a profusion of local shells. A path leads from the Grotto through the cliffside woods down some quite steep steps through several loggias to the shoreline pathway and the *Amis Réunis* stone boat.

GATE HOUSE

Gate House (1954-55, listed Grade II, 1971) was Clough's first building at Portmeirion following the lifting of building restrictions after the war. It straddles the driveway a short distance beyond the old tollgate. Rather than clear a level site for the building Clough made use of the existing terrain, making a feature of the rugged rock formations upon which the Gate House has been constructed.

The deep arch, floodlit at night, contains a ceiling mural by Hans Feibusch. The random pattern of fenestration, one chimney and many swags give Gate House a very Baroque character. The illusion of shutters to the upper floor windows is created by lines cut in the render and painted green.

During the 1960s Gate House was often taken for the summer season by Brian Epstein, manager of the Beatles; the wardrobe in the main bedroom was actually built at his request and to his own specifications.

BELVEDERE

The Belvedere (1960, listed Grade II, 1971) is a simple Classical house of two storeys with plain pilasters and a balcony over a recessed arched porch. It was designed in 1960 and built the same year. On the original drawing it is called the Fountain House but, as Anchor and Fountain already existed, Clough changed this to Belvedere, justifying the name because 'it occupies the premier view-point in all Portmeirion.' In front of Belvedere is a balustraded viewing platform overlooking the road.

Clough incorporated a stained glass window from Castell Deudraeth in the Belvedere's kitchen/dining room. It was made for David Williams, MP (1799-1869), attorney, landowner and first Liberal Member of Parliament for Merioneth. David Williams bought Castell Deudraeth, then called Bron Eryri, in 1841 and substantially rebuilt it as a castellated mansion. His motto 'Nid Da onid Duw' translates as 'No Good without God'.

BRIDGE HOUSE

Bridge House (1959, listed Grade II, 1971) forms the second of Portmeirion's two entrance gateways. A Classical building of early 18th century character the main façade faces south, its Rusticated podium pierced by a basket arch. It has Doric pilasters with cornice and coping topped by four tall urns. To the rear it has one large Venetian ogee arched window from Arnos Court with diamond panes.

As with Gate House, Clough fully exploited the existing terrain: the building rises on exposed brick arches from the living rock on both sides of the road. He described it as 'a classical thing, meticulously detailed, known locally as Carlton House Terrace.'

His later works were not necessarily intended to match up with earlier structures, but rather to provide 'piquant contrasts whereby both old and new would gain in interest. Thus, where I judged that I had perhaps a trifle overplayed the picturesque, I would pop in a bland façade of serene classical formality: for example, the village aspect of the Bridge House as seen beyond the shamelessly picturesque front of the black weather-boarded Toll House.'

TOLL HOUSE

Toll House (1929, listed Grade II, 1971) is of ancient character with oversailing upper storeys faced with weatherboarding. At the rear, seaward side, there is a lookout tower at the top floor level. Clough called Toll House 'that black weather boarded thing, looking rather Norwegian.'

It is embellished with plaques, bells and signs including an oak painted statue of St Peter on a balcony with a small canopy above his head (it would have been bigger but for a mistake at the foundry, but Clough thought St Peter would not mind). The bell was to summon the gatekeeper, and the blue and white striped pole could be lowered to restrict access - in 1929 this was the outer limit of the village.

The most striking embellishment is Susan Williams-Ellis's sheep cut-out which Clough asked her to design for the Welsh Wool Shop. Clough's original half-scale drawing dated March 1957 and Susan's finished full scale artwork have survived and are now in the Town Hall. She painted several murals for her father, most notably on the Salutation and on Lady's Lodge, as well as a plaque on Neptune.

BATTERY

Battery (1927, listed Grade II, 1971) was designed as 'Block C' on a plan dated 21 March 1927. It is of 18th century Kentish character with three storeys, the ground floor stuccoed with one lunette window, and weatherboarded above with wide eaves. In an article on Portmeirion by E. Maxwell Fry in the *Architects' Journal* of 20 June 1928, he described the Battery as 'a severer house painted all in white [that] looked calmly out over the waters, as though oblivious to the tower now rising from its tangle of scaffold poles to eclipse the authority of the first born.'

Clough justified the name Battery by having a couple of little cannons placed to guard its battlemented terrace. These were from Belan Fort, built on the Menai Strait to repel Napoleon's expected invasion.

CHART ROOM

Chart Room (1927) was originally a ground floor garage for use by the occupants of Battery. Many of Clough's cottages of the 1920s and 1930s had garages on the ground floor but they tended to be too small for post-war cars which anyhow no longer needed covered parking. From 1953 onwards these spaces were converted into shops or additional accommodation by Susan and her husband Euan Cooper-Willis in order to improve the village's viability. In this instance the space was made into a family room. The Plaque on the wall outside Chart Room is a piece of concrete statuary cast from a clay mould and titled 'Sculpture' by Gilbert Bayes. It is one of three displayed at the British Empire Exhibition and illustrated in *The Builder* (9 January 1925).

PILOT HOUSE

Pilot House (1930, listed Grade II 1971) was built to connect Toll House and Battery in the same weather boarded seaside style as Battery. It has wide metal framed windows overlooking the estuary and consists of two suites, one above the other. Like many buildings at Portmeirion it has a vaguely nautical name.

PRIOR'S LODGING

Prior's Lodging (1929, listed Grade II, 1971) is a small cottage of two storeys with sprocket eaves and a pantile roof. The seaward side has three tall narrow round headed windows from floor to ceiling. The ground floor originally housed a garage. Above this, through a baroque Italian doorway, from Clough's old London studio, is further accommodation. The front door is one of three acquired by Clough (another is at Plas Brondanw and the third at Castle Yard).

Clough explained that the rather pious-sounding name came about 'because its first tenant twenty-five years ago chanced to be the Prior of the Monastery set on the charming island of Caldy off the Pembroke coast.'

THE BELL TOWER

The Bell Tower, or the Campanile, was built in 1928 (listed Grade II, 1971). This was one of the few buildings at Portmeirion for which he prepared a complete half-inch drawing and stuck to it. A bell tower had been an integral feature of his early plans for Portmeirion, intended to draw attention to his venture: 'it was imperative that I should open my performance with a dramatic gesture of some sort.'

The Campanile housed an old turret clock from a demolished London brewery, and for many years the chiming of its bells marked the hour at Portmeirion.

A plaque at the base of the Tower reads: 'This tower, built in 1928 by Clough Williams-Ellis, architect and publican, embodies stones from the 12th century castle of his ancestor Gruffydd ap Cynan, King of North Wales, that stood on an eminence 150 yards to the west. It was finally razed c. 1869 by Sir William Fothergill Cook [sic], inventor of the Electric Telegraph, "lest the ruins should become known and attract visitors to the place." This 19th century affront to the 12th is thus piously redressed in the 20th.'

GOVERNMENT HOUSE

Government House (1928-29, listed Grade II, 1971) adjoined the earlier Watch House and the Campanile. It is of 18th century character with plastered walls, sprocket eaves and hipped roofs of pantiles. The Dolphin is joined to it by a loggia bridge at first floor level. Government House is so called because when it was built it dominated the whole then existing group upon the cliff top.

On the south-facing elevation there is a ceramic ship ornament and a trompe l'oeil window with a horned head looking out upon Battery lawn. Above the front door is a small sun peeping through the clouds and on the apex of the main tower is a copper seagull looking out to sea.

WATCH HOUSE

Watch House (1925-26, listed Grade II, 1971) is a small single-storey building of vernacular cottage character. A hipped slate roof (c.1963) replaced earlier pantiles. It has a very tall round chimney with a conical cap. The seaward end is built out on columns as a loggia. Watch House was an integral part of Clough's early concept of a group of buildings surrounding a tower on the cliff top and work was already in progress on the site by January 1926.

Descending from the Watch House to the sea is a series of steep walled steps and loggias (1927; listed Grade II) reminiscent of southern European castles or monasteries. The walls are of stone painted white and the loggias have pantile roofs.

THE DOLPHIN

Dolphin (1933-34, listed Grade II, 1971) was designed in July 1933, although the name itself had briefly been intended for what became known as the Angel. Dolphin is reached via a flight of steps down from Battery Square or up from the Dolphin wishing well. A loggia at first floor level connects Dolphin to Government House. Leaning over its seaward balcony is a ceramic bust of Shakespeare best seen from the quayside.

A carved Portland stone figure of the goddess Friga executed between 1728 and 1730 by Michael Rysbrack (1694-1770) stands on an integrally carved square plinth inscribed 'FRIX', and a square limestone pedestal. This figure was in situ here by at least 1928 and gives her name to Friday Lane past Mermaid. Clough wrote: 'There had been a circle of seven such deities severally representing the days of the week, but at a much earlier sale the then Duke of Buckingham, a most splendid bankrupt, had sold off the other six, leaving only mine - who, representing Friday, was presumably deemed unlucky and attracted no bidders.'

THE ROUND HOUSE

The Round House (1959-60, listed Grade II, 1971) is one of a pair of Baroque shops linked by an overhead walkway. The concept of a bow-fronted gate house and archway was already present in the model of his 'ideal village'. In 1934 Clough rebuild Cornwell Manor and village centre in Oxfordshire; the village hall he designed in 1938 bears similarity to the Round House.

In 1966 Patrick McGoohan used the Round House as Number Six's residence in *The Prisoner*. All interiors, however, were filmed at the MGM studios, Borehamwood, the Round House itself being too small to accommodate a spacious lounge, bedroom, bathroom and kitchen - a fact that can come as a surprise to visitors who know it from the television series. The building now houses Number Six, the Prisoner Shop. Clough wrote: 'Patrick McGoohan's ingenious and indeed mysterious television series *The Prisoner* stands alone for its revealing presentation of the place. When seen in colour at the local cinema, a performance he kindly arranged, Portmeirion itself seemed, to me, at least, to steal the show from its human cast.'

LADY'S LODGE

Lady's Lodge (1938-39, listed Grade II, 1971) was probably the last pre-war building at Portmeirion. Originally built as a lock-up garage it is one of a pair of Baroque shops with stuccoed walls, pantiled roof and small shop windows of Georgian character. The gables are shaped with scroll sides. The semi-circular mural above the bay window is by Hans Feibusch. Susan contributed a Byzantine coronation mural in 1956, but this has not survived and the alcove was later opened to form a window.

On conversion to a shop in the early 1960s it was called Battery Stores and then the Peacock. Both signs are featured in *The Prisoner*. This was the village shop in the series, though again the interiors were filmed in Metro-Goldwyn-Mayer studios at Borehamwood.

Below Lady's Lodge is a lead sundial in the shape of a cherub (listed Grade II in 1971).

THE PANTHEON

The Pantheon or Dome (1960-61, listed Grade II, 1971) is an octagonal building surmounted by a dome and central octagonal cupola. In the late-1950s Clough felt the village suffered from 'dome deficiency' and decided to remedy this. The foundation stone was laid by Earl Russell. For its ornate gothic porch he used a vast fireplace of red Runcorn sandstone from Dawpool, Cheshire which he had acquired 20 years previously. The supporting walls were built by April 1959 leaving only the actual dome itself. 'In the matter of the dome and its lantern,' he wrote, 'I just gave [Mr Braund-Smith, the master-joiner] the outside silhouette of what I wanted and left him to puzzle out its actual construction: a challenge met with an economy and elegance that is in itself a pleasure to behold.'

As the ball was finally fixed on top of the Dome, Clough could be seen high up a ladder (he was nearing eighty at the time) laying on the gold leaf. The Pantheon is assumed by many to be a temple and Clough was often under pressure to make it over for such use but, as his own position was firmly neutral, he saw its future as probably secular.

THE CHANTRY

The Chantry (1937, listed Grade II, 1971) was so christened simply because Clough happened to like the name. The first phase of building at Portmeirion involved Clough in 'pegging out' the project by committing himself to the essential dominant structures, to be linked up with less important buildings later. Thus was Chantry conceived and built at the highest point of all, an escarpment of rock sheer above the roadway and village green. It was intended for Augustus John and included a studio for him on the top floor, complete with fish eye lens looking out over the Campanile. Augustus John, however, had other plans.

The panel on the cupola is a carving in blue and gold of Sun and Glory.

VILLA WINCH

Villa Winch (1966-67) is located behind Chantry Cottage and is linked to it by a pantiled archway. A design for the Winch survives from April 1966 together with a revised version dated June 1966. A cottage for Captain Henry Winch, a neighbour, had been in the planning for some time, comprising a semi-circular studio and roof terrace overlooking the estuary. The building might have been intended for where the Grotto now stands. This rather more modest version was the one that was built in the end. The round windows are *trompe l'oeil*.

CHANTRY ROW

Chantry Row (1962-63, listed Grade II, 1971) was designed in February 1962 and built to link Chantry Cottage to the Pantheon. It is one single-storey building arranged to simulate a terrace of four houses, each painted a different colour and with dummy attic windows. Clough had toyed with the idea of building two similar rows to flank the new Piazza but in the end only actually included the Gloriette. There is a viewpoint in front of Chantry Row which features one of the eight Ionic columns that Clough had acquired in the 1930s.

The Onion Dome on Chantry Row was designed not only to add interest but also to hide an unsightly chimney. It consists of half an octagonal turret with half dome painted green in imitation of copper. Seen from behind it is simply a façade, as the design illustrates. However, as Clough liked to point out, it was only supposed to be seen from the front.

THE PIAZZA

The Piazza (1965, pool and fountain listed Grade II, 1971) had originally been considered in 1925, but that particular design was not executed. However in the early-1960s he was encouraged by Susan and Euan to create the central Piazza; it was pointed out that the tennis court could be re-sited in a less sensitive position close to the entrance to the village.

His first drawing for the Piazza is dated 1963 and included two rows of cottages similar to Chantry Row and a tower. Although detailed drawings of the tower exist it was not built: only the Gloriette facing a shallow pond containing a fountain, and steps between two Ionic columns down to the Gothic Pavilion, were included. His plans had to be postponed for some time as he wanted to use seven Ionic Columns which he had acquired thirty years before but could not find. The Ionic columns are adorned with gilded Burmese dancing figures in the style associated with late 19th century court arts of Mandalay, marked by the flamboyant treatment of costume details, especially the exaggerated play of the flame motif.

THE GLORIETTE

The Gloriette (1964-65, listed Grade II, 1971) was designed in 1963 as part of the Piazza development but of this only the fountain and portico were kept. The portico was revised in 1964 and renamed the Gloriette, after the purely spectacular classical confection that closes the great vista at the Schönbrunn Palace near Vienna. Clough's purpose here was to provide a piquant contrast whereby both old and new would gain in interest: 'the Palladian Gloriette vivaciously contradicts the more sober, old, converted stable block across the way.'

It derives from his rescue in the 1930s of the Colonnade by Samuel Wyatt (1737-1807) at Hooton Hall in Cheshire, including eight massive Ionic columns. 'For nearly thirty years I forgot all about this rather rash and extravagant purchase until I had my Gloriette idea by which time these bits and pieces could nowhere be found. Ultimately they were tracked down and actually dug up from under a garden that had been made on top of them.'

THE BRISTOL COLONNADE

The Colonnade (built, c.1760, rebuilt here 1959, listed Grade II, 1971) was opened by Earl Russell on 10 April 1959. Its dedicatory inscription reads as follows: 'This colonnade built circa 1760 by the Quaker copper smelter William Reeve, stood before his bathhouse at Arnos Court, Bristol. Damaged by bombs it had fallen into decay and although scheduled as an Ancient Monument, Her Majesty's Minister of Works approved its removal on condition that it should be here re-scheduled.'

A precise measured survey made by a Bristol architect survives, showing every single stone, each numbered on the drawing as well as on itself. Clough's master mason, William Davies, took over all the papers along with the stone heaps and set about the resurrection. As Clough recalled, 'First to last, in Bristol as well as at Portmeirion, it was almost entirely a matter of high masonic craft, for, having determined its site and fixed its levels, there was little more for me to do but look on, approve and very much admire.'

GOTHIC PAVILION

The Gothic Pavilion (1965, listed Grade II, 1971) was built to front the Gloriette beyond its pool and fountain. Like the Gloriette, it was built from salvaged material. Clough writes: 'This was a generous gift to me from Nerquis Hall in Flintshire, where as a *porte cochère* it was deemed to be an excrescence on an otherwise distinguished and authentic Jacobean façade - as indeed it was.' Unfortunately the pavilion was badly damaged during its dismantling. 'In fact, had I not been blessed with inspired masons, I should have just heaped the pieces into a rockery. As it was, we went bravely ahead, and in the end built up, not the original portico, but an amended version which with its more attenuated proportions and slender pinnacles is generally held to have gained in elegance whatever it may have lost in authenticity.'

A pair of barley twist teak columns support painted metal cutouts, which, like the Onion Dome were to be viewed from the front only.

MERMAID

The Mermaid (c. 1840, 'Clough-ed up' 1926, listed Grade II, 1971) is one of four buildings in the village to pre-date Clough's involvement (the others being the Salutation, the Hotel and White Horses). It was used as a gardener's bothy between 1842 and 1858. Fronting the Mermaid is a wishing well adorned with a group of copper dolphins. A slate plaque carries the following dedication: 'The Dolphin Group was presented by the staff of Portmeirion to C W-E CBE in affectionate regard on the occasion of his 80th birthday.'

Clough added the south facing tent shaped Regency canopy supported on trellaced iron columns as well as the canopy and statue to the north gable.

The term to 'Clough-up' was first coined to describe his treatment of this traditional building, exemplified by these additions and the use of contrasting colours. The scalloped barge-boards are original however and were also used on the hotel building according to early photographs. The white figure is Charity, a wooden statue of the late 17th or early 18th century, possibly by Gabriel Grupello (1644-1730).

THE BAND STAND

The Bandstand was designed and built in 1961 as the 'Portmeirion Substation superstructure loggia' to house and ultimately disguise the village's electrical submains station, for which it is used to this day. The mermaid panels used here, as well as elsewhere in the village, are from the Sailors' Home in Liverpool which Clough had acquired as a job lot for next to nothing at the time when that venerable institution was demolished in 1954. These panels can also be seen on the Gloriette, the Bridge House, Gazebo, Anchor balustrade and inside the Pantheon. One stray panel is located on Gwynedd Council Offices and another in Pont Street in London, at one time the site of a Portmeirion antiques shop.

THE ANGEL

The Angel (1926, listed Grade II, 1971) was one of Clough's first cottages at Portmeirion. It was so called because Clough had an attractive Angel sign which he wanted to use. Its design dates from late 1925 or early 1926 and the cottage was built at the same time as Neptune ('the Garage Block'). These two cottages are referred to as 'Block A' and 'Block B' on Clough's early drawings.

In style the Angel is traditional West country vernacular with virtually no straight sides or right angles. The materials are specified as 9-inch brickwork on the ground floor, 4-inch studding faced with cement plaster on the first floor, and Crittall's metal casement windows. On Angel's south terrace Clough erected an Astrolabe to commemorate the introduction of Summer Time. The citation round the circular seat reads simply, 'To William Willett, in gratitude.' William Willett was instrumental in establishing Summer Time and daylight-saving and Clough believed we should be grateful to the man who gave us our long summer evenings.

NEPTUNE

Neptune (1926, listed Grade II, 1971) and Angel were Clough's first cottages at Portmeirion, but which came first is unclear. His drawing for Neptune, dated Oct. 1925 calls Neptune 'Block A' and Angel 'Block B.' Its siting alongside Mermaid cottage directly in front of the existing pool suggests that Neptune may have come first. They were certainly conceived as a pair and their construction was probably more or less simultaneous. Both were in situ by the end of 1926 and in use as additional hotel accommodation. Neptune was called 'the Garage Block' on early plans and provided space for seven cars. These garages were converted into a shop in the early 1960s, now the Golden Dragon Bookshop.

TRINITY

Trinity (1933-34, listed Grade II, 1971) was so named because Clough happened to have that worshipful institution's coat-of-arms in cast iron, brought from an island lighthouse keeper's quarters. Trinity provided accommodation on the first and second floors and garage parking for three cars on the ground floor facing Trinity Yard. The garage was in due course converted into a shop (now called Pot Jam) and the irregular floor levels are a reminder of its previous use.

Facing the pool beneath arched alcoves are marble busts of the Duke and Duchess of Argyll by Michael Rysbrack (1694-1770). Clough irreverently placed them on pedestals made from upturned petrol cans.

A National Benzole petrol pump (1926) was installed outside Neptune, embellished with an elegant early 19th Century pine figurehead. Petrol was not widely available and this was therefore an essential facility next to the lock-up garages. The original figurehead was stolen in 1983 but turned up in the pages of *Country Life* in 1996 and was duly recovered at considerable expense.

SALUTATION

Salutation was originally the lodge and stable block at Aber Iâ (c.1850, listed Grade II, 1971). The roof of fish scale slates was a feature of the 19th century buildings here and can be seen on Mermaid and the Hotel. Salutation also has the same twisted chimneys as the hotel.

Clough adapted this stable block 'in a rather slapdash way' once he had completed Angel and Neptune. In 1966-67 he 'Cloughed-up' the right hand gable in a style similar to a Dutch gable. The building was first used as a cafe in 1931 when visitor numbers had overwhelmed the capacity of the hotel: 'The Salutation serves the passing traveller either in its black and white marble-floored Salle or else on one of its terraces, amongst clipped bay trees and flower urns beneath the shade of sycamores.'

As well as the Salutation Restaurant the building also housed the Ship Shop, which specialises in Portmeirion Pottery. Susan designed and painted a colourful mural of vines and cupids with fountain and white doves on the courtyard side of this building which, having been painted over, was recreated in 1996 by artist Nigel Simmons.

ARCHES

Arches (1963-64, listed Grade II, 1971) was first designed in July 1954 and was then known as Upper Arches House, before being revised in February 1956 and renamed the Arches). It is of Mediterranean village character and comprises three storeys and a dummy attic with an arcaded ground floor of three round headed arches.

It provided staff flats above three garage spaces. In 1965 the garages were converted into the Angel Arcade antiques shop run for many years by Sylvia Jones. The Angel Arcade mural was painted by Hans Feibusch.

Close to the Arches is a column built of bricks topped with a classical nymph. This is known as the Williams-Ellis column.

GAZEBO

The Gazebo (1983) was designed by Susan Williams-Ellis to mark the centenary of Clough's birth. This was officially opened by Sir Hugh Casson. The gazebo makes use of six of the 30 mermaid panels that Clough had acquired in 1954 from the Sailors' Home in Liverpool. Clough often said he hoped his descendants would give his village little presents and he would no doubt have approved of this one.

ANCHOR AND FOUNTAIN

Anchor (1936, listed Grade II, 1971) was designed in 1930. The Fountain (1937, listed Grade II) was designed sometime later. Clough's preliminary design for Anchor is unusual in showing the dramatic setting of the new building. This block was to stand against a cliff beside a lawn and cascade, at the lowest level in the village.

Access is by a bridge leading off the drive which passes it at eaves level. The constructional methods and details were kept as elementary as possible, since each new building had to be started when the hotel closed in the autumn and to be completed by the following Easter. Anchor comprised six small bedrooms which in 1990 were converted into three spacious suites. The mural of Neptune on Anchor is by Hans Feibusch. It was at Fountain that Noël Coward wrote *Blithe Spirit*.

THE TOWN HALL

The Town Hall (1937-38, listed Grade II, 1971), also known as Hercules Hall, was designed to house a Jacobean ceiling, panelling and mullioned windows salvaged from Emral in Flintshire. Fronting the Hall is a fine set of wrought iron gates dated 1908 between stucco piers topped by a cornice and urn (Listed Grade II). Emral Hall was one of the great houses of Wales, the central and oldest part (early 17th century), containing the remarkable barrel-vaulted plaster ceiling depicting the labours of Hercules.

In the mid-1930s Clough noticed an item in *Country Life* announcing the demolition of Emral Hall. 'Aghast at the news I rang up the National Trust: too late and no money. Then the V&A Museum: no room. So I felt I must instantly do something about it myself: packed a bag, caught a train, and reached Emral just as the sale was starting...So far as the ballroom section was concerned, the ceiling came up first, and there being next to no bidding for so awkward and speculative a lot, it was knocked down to me for a derisory thirteen pounds. But then of course I had to buy all the rest of the room at any cost; the old leaded glass in its mullioned windows, its fire grate, its oak cornices and architraves - the lot. And committed that far, it was but prudent to buy a great deal more of the old house wherewith to contrive an apt new building in which to embed my reconstructed ballroom. Whence the somewhat hybrid aspect of what is now Portmeirion's Town Hall, an unabashed pastiche of venerable Jacobean bits and pieces adding interest and dignity, as I think, to an otherwise straightforward modern structure.'

Clough's foreman joiner, RO Williams reinforced the ceiling from behind and, having numbered and sawn it into a hundred sections, lowered each one into straw lined crates.

The lantern on top of the building is surmounted by an ornate copper crown on top of an upturned pig boiler.

TRIUMPHAL ARCH

The Triumphal Arch (1962-63, listed Grade II, 1971) was built at the suggestion of Clough's daughter Susan and her husband Euan who pointed out that a new way in was needed for delivery lorries unable to pass under the Gate House and Bridge House arches. Clough was not keen but when a Triumphal Arch was mentioned immediately became interested and drew a sketch of a Rococo style gateway with rusticated arch beneath a high pediment inscribed by two massive scrolls.

The statue in the arch is an early 19th century wooden model for a series of lead Caryatids illustrated in *Weaver's English Leadwork* (1909) with the note: 'On a balcony of a house in Park Lane are lead Caryatids, and very graceful they are with their windswept draperies. They were erected about eighty years ago, and their great weight nearly pulled down the whole balcony.' The Mermaid shields were cast in concrete. To the left of the Triumphal Arch is a small piazza (1962-63, listed Grade II, 1971) with four Classical caryatids and dolphin fountain. Close by is a Chinoiserie wrought iron ornament which fronts the main path into the Gwyllt.

TELFORD'S TOWER

Telford's Tower (1958, listed Grade II, 1971) was built to mark Thomas Telford's bi-centenary. It is an 'L' shaped stucco building with an oriel window at its base and a shingle roof with vase finial. Its interiors are finely detailed. A concrete spiral staircase leads up to tower bedrooms.

Between Telford and Unicorn a flight of steps leads through an arch embellished with a high relief lion and unicorn coat of arms to an empty space where Clough had proposed to site his final building at Portmeirion, to be called the Lion Tower. He said in an interview with Peter Davey (11 February 1973), 'There is just one tower I want to add between Telford's Tower and the Unicorn.'

UNICORN

Unicorn (1964, listed Grade II, 1971) is a Palladian house with seven windows and four Doric pilasters with a pediment over embellished with a Unicorn. This and Bridge House are the village's most prosperous Georgian-looking houses and both share a light classic style.

Clough on occasions named Unicorn his favourite building at Portmeirion as it embodied his belief that good design need not cost more. This 'mini Chatsworth' as it was sometimes called is set back above the roadway in imposing isolation but its grandeur is deflated by a peek around the back. This reveals it to be a flat roofed bungalow. The mermaid panel to the front of the balcony is one of around thirty that Clough got from the Sailors' Home in Liverpool.

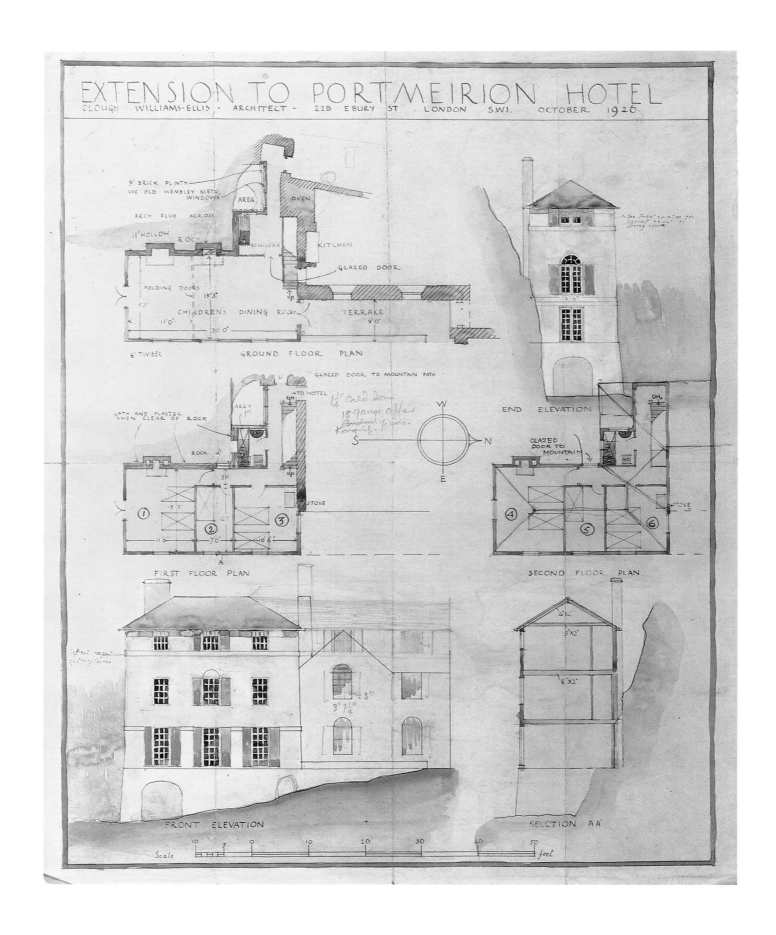

EXTENSION TO PORTMEIRION HOTEL

CLOUGH WILLIAMS-ELLIS · ARCHITECT · 22B EBURY ST LONDON S.W.1. OCTOBER 1926

9" BRICK PLINTH
USE OLD WEMBLEY METAL WINDOWS
ARCH FLUE ACROSS
11" HOLLOW ROCK
AREA
OVEN
SCULLERY
KITCHEN
GLAZED DOOR
FOLDING DOORS
13'3"
5'3"
CHILDREN'S DINING ROOM
11'0"
30'0"
TERRACE 8'0"
6" TIMBER

GROUND FLOOR PLAN

GLAZED DOOR TO MOUNTAIN PATH

LATH AND PLASTER WHEN CLEAR OF ROCK
AREA 11"
TO HOTEL
ROCK
W
N
S
E
ROCK
3'0"
dp
① 13'3"
② 7'0" 12'0"
③ 10'6"
11'6"
STOVE
A

FIRST FLOOR PLAN

END ELEVATION

GLAZED DOOR TO MOUNTAIN
DN
④
⑤
⑥
STOVE
WC

SECOND FLOOR PLAN

16'6"

FRONT ELEVATION

3' 7½"
+5"

SECTION AA'

4"x2"
5"x2"
8"x2"

Scale   10   5   0   10   20   30   40   50   feet

AMIS REUNIS

The *Amis Réunis* (1930) is neither building nor ship, rather it is a bit of both.

Almost as soon as Portmeirion opened in 1926 Clough bought and converted a graceful old Porthmadog trading ketch of some seventy tons which he moored alongside the quay. This he used as a houseboat with water and electricity laid on. During a sudden gale with a spring tide under her and anchors trailing she was carried out towards the island, Ynys Gifftan, and there stranded on a down-sloping shoal so that when the tide ebbed she lay on her beam ends, her masts nearly horizontal and her keel in the air.

Having failed to save her, and being at that time engaged in building the new quay to replace the shale bank below the hotel, Clough noticed that the quay's end followed almost exactly the line of the ship's bulwarks and resolved to reconstruct her as a ship-aground. Sections of her mainmast act as pillars supporting the dining room's flat roof.

The hotel lawn balustrading and its Coade stone statues are original Victorian features which Clough embellished in 1930 with an elegant quayside loggia called the Casino.

THE HOTEL

The Hotel (1850, extended 1926 & 1930; listed Grade II, 1971) was the original mansion of Aber Iâ. It was built around 1850 and was first described by Richard Richards in 1861 as 'one of the most picturesque of all the summer residences to be found on the sea-coast of Wales.'

Clough's first extension of the house was drawn in 1926. This tower-like wing on the west of the old house rises close to the cliff face. The wing was originally limewashed with yellow, and its subtlety depends on the use of external window shutters painted in the green which became synonymous with the village. Clough added a new dining room in 1930. Instead of reproducing the Victorian style of the original structure, here Clough exploited a curved, highly glazed plan of Modernist concept.

Clough later added a new entrance and offices in a similar style around 1935. These additions to the front of the hotel continued in use until their destruction in the fire of 1981. Conceived as superimposed glazed walls on curved plans under flat roofs, they were fluent and modern spaces, which enabled the functions of a hotel to coexist with a Victorian house hemmed in by a cliff.

Following the 1981 fire, reconstruction was in time achieved with the main rooms substantially restored to their former state as evidenced by Clough's description of the original interior: 'As you enter the hall past a massive carved Italian Renaissance fireplace, you see beyond it the wide and easy flight of a typical 18th century stair with an elegant balustrade. No one knows whence it came, but we do know where the library at its foot came from, and it was the Great Exhibition of 1851 - all complete with its intricately carved doors and mantelpiece - to be built straight into the house that was then, presumably, just ready to receive it.

'The Mirror Room, next to it, reflects as you enter the view outside the wrong way round; the mantelshelf is supported by the functional haloes of a pair of carved saints and the inlaid parquet is that surviving the room's use as a curs' kennel - strangely without a mark. The big room at the end of the hall was originally the billiards room - pleasant enough with a bay window towards the sea and a wide alcove opposite. It was the dining room when the house first became an hotel and so continued until I built out a new curvilinear one beyond it.'

THE OBSERVATORY TOWER

The Observatory Tower (1936-37, listed Grade II, 1971) was designed in October 1935. A Camera Obscura said to have been from a German U-Boat was installed in the tower in 1939 as noted in the 'Stop Press' section of the Fourth Edition of the Guide Book (April 1939): 'A camera obscura is being installed at the top of the new lighthouse by the White Horses at the end of the old quay.'

The architectural form of the Observatory Tower has Clough's characteristic forced perspective and scaled-down detail to increase its apparent size. It is now surmounted by a star; the plan shows a cut-out of a mermaid on a globe, which was made but which did not survive the frequent coastal gales and is now sited at the old tollgate near the entrance.

At the foot of the Observatory Tower is a Coade stone figure of Nelson (listed Grade II, 1971), given to Clough by Sir Michael Duff of Y Faenol near Caernarfon. Next to it is a weeping beech given to Clough by his friends on his 80th birthday.

WHITE HORSES

White Horses (part 18th century, extended 1966; listed Grade II, 1971) was originally a fisherman's cottage. The old part is a single storey stone building with central chimney stack of traditional Welsh pattern. Clough's addition links the Observatory Tower to the old cottage. It is constructed on arches over the path which overlooks an inset anchorage for boats.

The cottage was inhabited for a time by Thomas Edwards, an infamous South Walian better known locally as yr Hwntw Mawr who worked as a labourer for William Maddocks. In 1813 he was publicly hanged at Dolgellau for the murder of Mary Jones, the maid at Penrhyn Isaf farm close to Portmeirion.

White Horses is so called because with a spring tide and a south-westerly gale, crested breakers batter its walls and occasionally even break and enter. At one time Clough used it as a workshop where weaving and dyeing went on. In 1966 he converted it into habitable accommodation by adding two bedrooms raised on arches. One of the first residents was Patrick McGoohan who stayed at White Horses during the filming of *The Prisoner*.

THE LIGHTHOUSE

Further along the coast one comes to a folly lighthouse which marks Portmeirion's southernmost point. Made of sheet metal and crowned with an upturned pig boiler and ornate finial it was in situ by 1963.

BIBLIOGRAPHY

WORKS BY CLOUGH WILLIAMS-ELLIS

Architect Errant (Constable, London, 1971)

Around the World in Ninety Years (Golden Dragon, Portmeirion, 1978)

Britain and the Beast (JM Dent, London, 1937), edited by Clough Willims-Ellis

England and the Octopus (Geoffrey Bles, London, 1928; reprinted with new preface Golden Dragon, Portmeirion, 1975)

Plan for Living: The Architect's Part (Faber & Faber, London, 1941)

'Planning and Propaganda' in *Labour Monthly: A Magazine of International Labour*, vol. 24 no.2, February 1942 – Clough & Amabel Williams-Ellis

The Pleasures of Architecture (Cape, London, 1924) – Clough & Amabel Williams-Ellis

'Portmeirion' in *Town Planning Review* (University Press of Liverpool, 1931)

Portmeirion: The Place and its Meaning (Faber & Faber, London, 1963; reprinted with additional illustrations Portmeirion Ltd, Portmeirion, 2006)

'Soviet Architecture' in *Left Review*, vol.3 no.10, November 1937

WORKS BY OTHER AUTHORS

In addition to contemporary newspapers and magazines, the following have been consulted by the authors:

Nicholas Blake, *Malice in Wonderland* (Collins, London, 1940)

Andrew Casey, *20th Century Ceramic Designers in Britain* (Antique Collectors' Club, Suffolk, 2001)

Andrew Casey, *Starting to Collect 20th Century Ceramics* (Antique Collectors' Club, Suffolk, 2006)

Andrew Casey and Ann Eatwell (ed.), *Susie Cooper: A Pioneer of Modern Design* (Antique Collectors' Club, Suffolk, 2002)

James Chapman, *Saints & Avengers: British Adventure Series of the 1960s* (IB Tauris, London, 2002)

Ronald W Clark, *The Life of Bertrand Russell* (Penguin, Harmondsworth, 1978)

John Coldstream, *Dirk Bogarde* (Weidenfeld & Nicholson, London, 2004)

Euan Cooper-Willis, *The World of Botanic Garden 1972–1997* (Portmeirion Potteries Ltd, Stoke-on-Trent, 1997)

John Cornforth, 'Portmeirion Revisited' in *Country Life* (16 & 23 September, 1976)

Andy Croft, *Red Letter Days: British Fiction in the 1930s* (Lawrence & Wishart, London, 1990)

Catherine Németh Frumerman, *On the Trail of the Prisoner: A Walking Guide to Portmeirion's Prisoner Sites* (PrizBiz, www.priz.biz, 2003)

E Maxwell Fry, 'Port Meirion' in *The Architects' Journal* (20 June 1928)

Edward Hallam, *Ashtead Potters Ltd in Surrey* (Hallam Publishing, Surrey, 1990)

Richard Haslam, *Clough Williams-Ellis* (Academy Editions, London, 1996)

Richard Haslam, 'Wales's Universal Architect' in *Country Life* (21 July, 1983)

Leslie Hayward, *Poole Pottery: Carter & Company 1873-2002* (Richard Dennis, Somerset, 2002)

Desmond Heap, *An Outline of the New Planning Law* (Sweet & Maxwell, London, 1949)

Christopher Hussey, 'Large Ideas for Small Estates' in *Country Life* (5 April, 1930)

Steven Jenkins & Stephen P McKay, *Portmeirion Pottery* (Richard Dennis, Somerset, 2000)

Jonah Jones, *Clough Williams-Ellis* (Seren, Bridgend, 1996)

Robert Langley, *The Prisoner in Portmeirion* (Portmeirion Ltd, Portmeirion, 1999)

Griselda Lewis, *A Collectors' History of English Pottery* (Antique Collectors' Club, Suffolk, 5th edn 1999)

John and Griselda Lewis, *Pratt Ware 1780–1840* (Antique Collectors' Club, Suffolk, 2005)

Jon E Lewis & Penny Stempel, *Cult TV: The Essential Critical Guide* (Pavilion, London, 1993)

Robin Llywelyn, *Portmeirion* (Gomer Press, Ceredigion, 2006)

Christopher Matthew, *A Different World: Stories of Great Hotels* (Paddington Press, London, 1976)

The Oxford Dictionary of National Biography (OUP, Oxford, 2004)

Portmeirion Guide Book (Portmeirion, 2000)

Raymond Postgate, *The Good Food Guide 1951-52* (Cassell & Co, London, 1951) and subsequent editions

Arnold Rattenbury, 'Time Packaged, Pyramid at Sea' in *The WH Auden Society Newsletter No. 8* (December 1991)

Victoria Stanton & Euan Cooper-Willis, *The Story of Portmeirion Potteries 1960– 1995* (Portmeirion Potteries, Stoke-on-Trent, 1995)

John St Loe Strachey, *The Adventure of Living* (Hodder & Stoughton, London, 1922)

Stefan Szczelkun, *The Conspiracy of Good Taste: William Morris, Cecil Sharp, Clough Williams-Ellis and the Repression of Working Class Culture in the 20th Century* (Working Press, London, 1993)

Alwyn W Turner, *Tribute: A Salute to the British Armed Forces of the Second World War* (St Lennard's Press, London, 1995)

Amabel Williams-Ellis, *Clough Williams-Ellis: A Portrait in Words* (Golden Dragon, Portmeirion, 1981)

Amabel Williams-Ellis, *All Stracheys are Cousins* (Weidenfeld & Nicholson, London, 1983)

INDEX

PICTURE CREDITS

All photographs and illustrations are courtesy of Portmeirion Ltd,
with the exception of the following:

CLOUGH'S PLANS AND DRAWINGS ON PAGES 12, 15, 20, 56, 110, 114, 218
AND 234 are the copyright of the Second Portmeirion Foundation;

IMAGES ON PAGES 1, 39, 41, 74, 88, 90, 100, 135 (pottery only) 138
(Moss Agate), 140, 145, 150–151 courtesy of Stephen McKay;

PHOTOGRAPHS ON PAGES 2, 66, 111, 129, 162, 184, 189, 199, 204, 206,
209 & 210 © Charles Hawes (www.veddw.co.uk);

MERYL WATTS PICTURES ON PAGES 74, 88 & 90 used by permission of the family
of the late Elizabeth Jane Graham;

PHOTOGRAPHS ON PAGES 102, 104 & 106 supplied by Roger Langley; no
reproduction without consent;

PHOTOGRAPHS ON PAGE 125 by Beth Evans, via Benchmark Woodworking Ltd;

PHOTOGRAPHS ON PAGES 130, 131 (LOGO) 134, 136–7, 139, 141–144, 146–149
& 152–159, 235 (wine list) supplied by Portmeirion Potteries Ltd.

Portmeirion Ltd photographs are by Bruno Poiret, Susan Williams-Ellis,
Mike McGregor, Edwin Smith, JR Greenwood, Sian Llywelyn, Peter Williams
(Image House Photography), Richard Tilbrook and Nigel Hughes
(Nigel Hughes Photography, Porthmadog).

*Efforts have been made to obtain all necessary permissions to reproduce images.
Any errors or omissions should be notified to the publisher and will be corrected
in future editions.*

ACKNOWLEDGEMENTS

The editors and authors would like to thank:
Sian Llwelyn of Portmeirion Shops Ltd; Arwel Hughes, Russell Sharp &
Mike McGregor at Portmeirion gardens; Merfyn Williams, Chairman of the
Second Portmeirion Foundation; Siôn Dobson Jones & Frank Stewart at the
Hotel Portmeirion, and Honor Williams at Castell Deudraeth; Bleddyn Griffiths,
Property & Grounds Manager at Portmeirion; Michael Haynes, Julian Teed,
Wayne Mountford, Andrew Stoddard, Gary Preston, Sharon McAvoy &
Carol Wright at Portmeirion Potteries; Sam Beazley for his memories of the
Village and the Pont Street shop; Andrew Casey; Griselda Lewis for her expertise
on Pratt Ware and pottery production techniques; Stephen McKay, who coined
the term *Portmeiriana* to describe Portmeirion-related artefacts, as well as giving
us access to his own collection; Roger Langley of the official Prisoner
appreciation society, Six of One (Box 66, Ipswich IP2 9TZ); Gwyn Davies at
Snowdonia Press, Porthmadog, for help with finding and copying images;
Dennis Buckingham; Roger Goodman; the editor of, and contributors to, the
bulletin boards at urban75.org; Francis King & Kevin Morgan at the Socialist
History Society, and Andy Croft.

We would also like to thank all the staff at the Antique Collectors' Club who in
their 40th Anniversary year helped in the production of this book, in particular:
Diana Steel, Tom Conway, Jane Enemy, Alison Hart, Juliet Henney,
Stephen Mackinlay, Anna Pearce, Sarah Smye, Craig Taylor and Richard Weale.

Finally, and above all, this book would have been impossible without the
time, support and enthusiasm of Robin Llywelyn, Susan Williams-Ellis and
Euan Cooper-Willis. They have our deepest gratitude.

©2006 Mark Eastment, Jools Holland, Stephen Lacey,
Robin Llywelyn, Jan Morris and Alwyn W Turner
World copyright reserved

ISBN 10: 1-85149-522-3
ISBN 13: 978-1-85149-522-1

The right of Mark Eastment, Jools Holland, Stephen Lacey,
Robin Llywelyn, Jan Morris and Alwyn W Turner to be identified
as authors of this work has been asserted by them in accordance
with the Copyright, Designs and Patents Act 1988

All rights reserved. No part of this publication may be reproduced, stored
in a retrieval system, or transmitted in any form or by any means electronic,
mechanical, photocopying, recording or otherwise, without the prior
permission of the publishers.

British Library Cataloguing-in-Publication Data
A catalogue record for this book is available from the British Library

Designed by Isobel Gillan

Printed in China
for the Antique Collectors' Club Ltd.,
Woodbridge, Suffolk

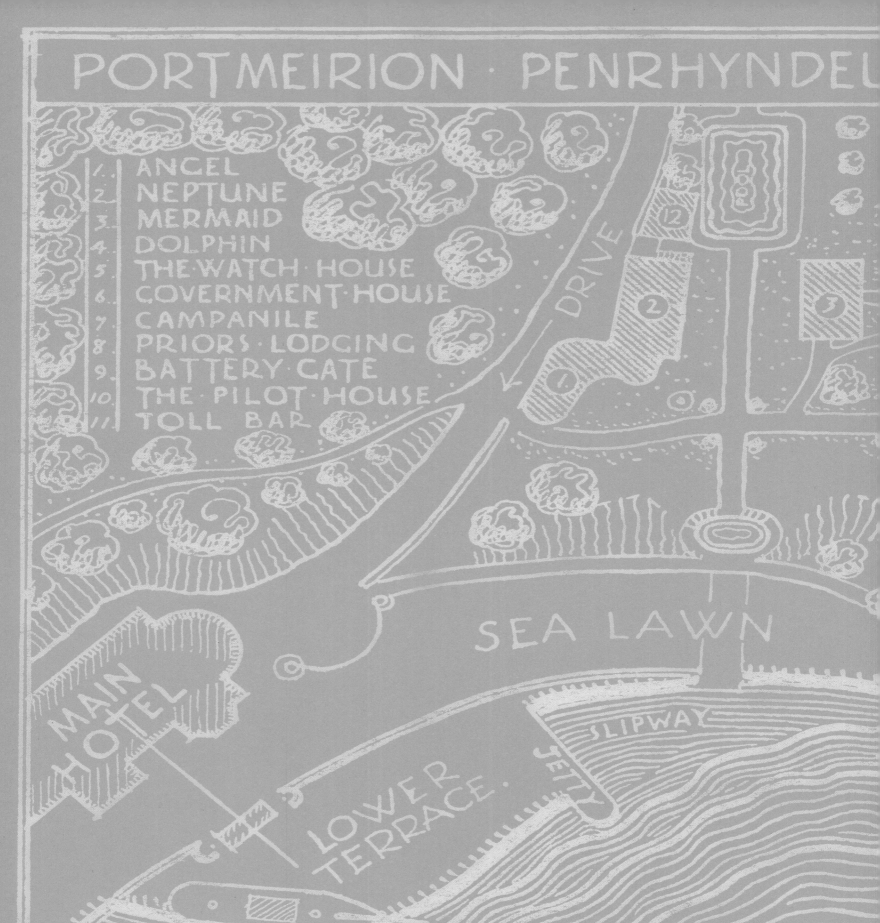

PORTMEIRION · PENRHYNDEU

1. ANGEL
2. NEPTUNE
3. MERMAID
4. DOLPHIN
5. THE WATCH HOUSE
6. GOVERNMENT HOUSE
7. CAMPANILE
8. PRIORS LODGING
9. BATTERY GATE
10. THE PILOT HOUSE
11. TOLL BAR

DRIVE

SEA LAWN

MAIN HOTEL

LOWER TERRACE

SLIPWAY

JETTY